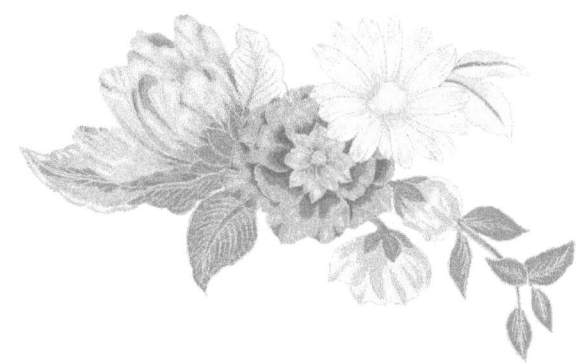

BELONGS TO

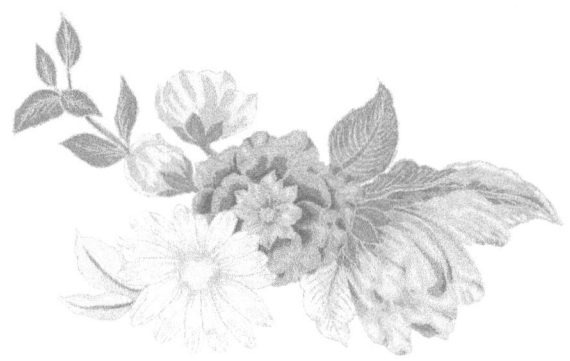

Coloring Book for Adults Relaxation

welcome to my happy and colorful world of Women Color Featuring.

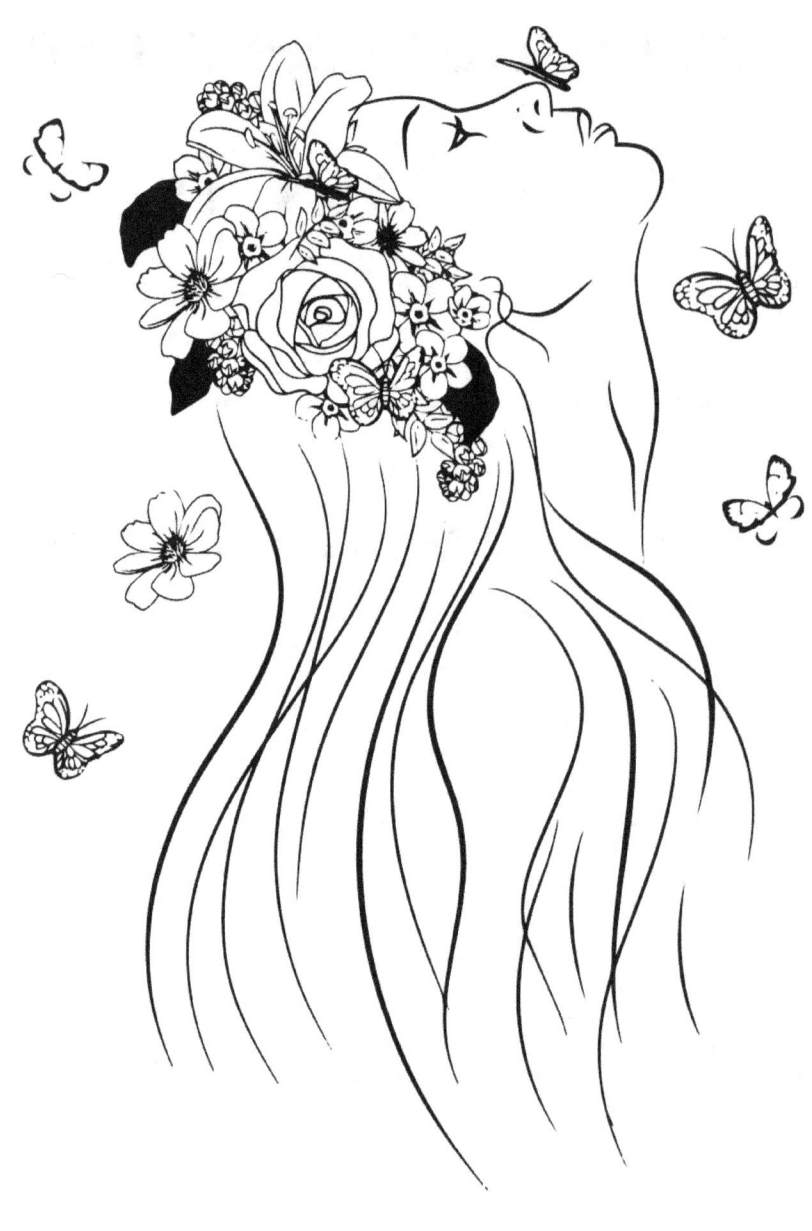

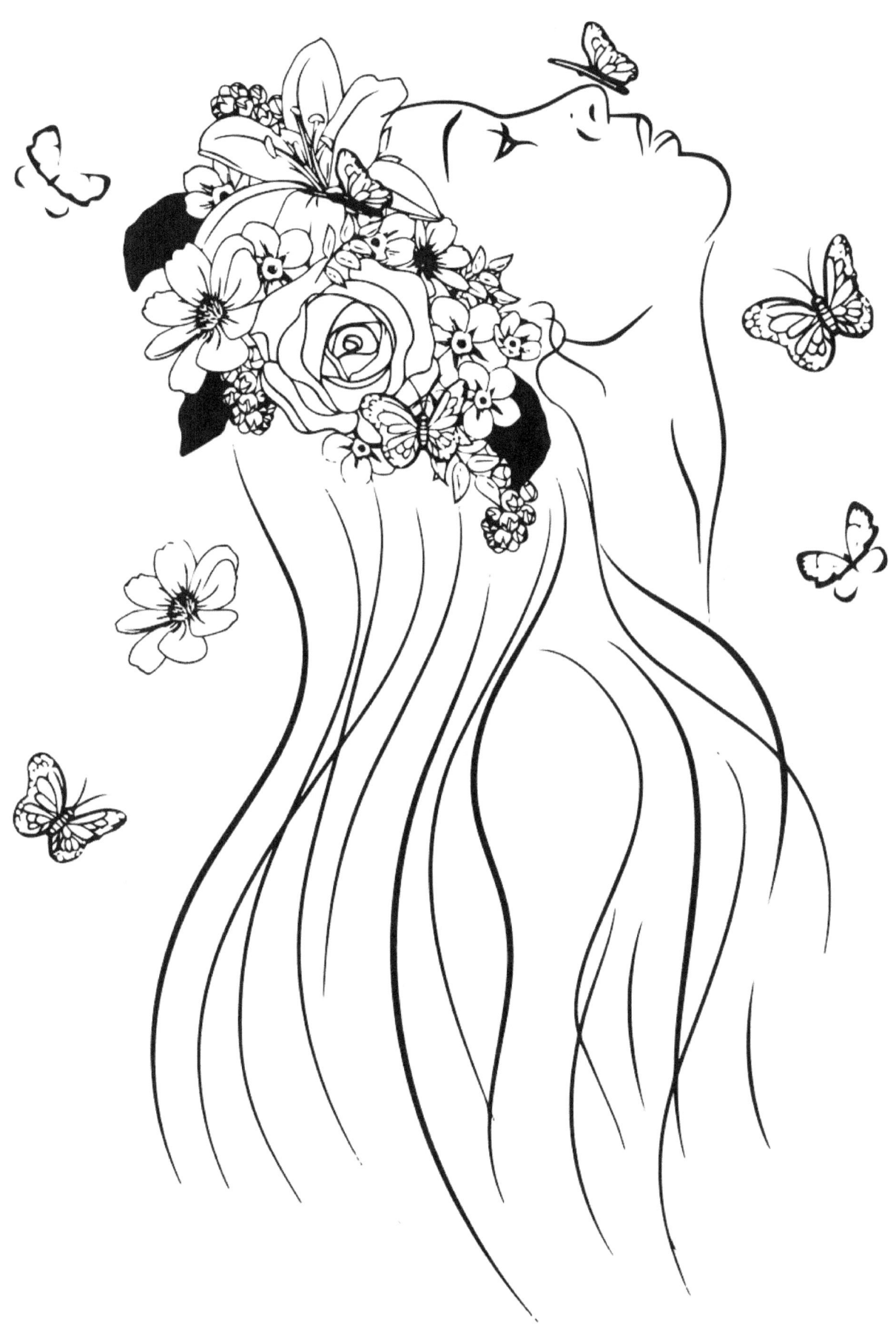

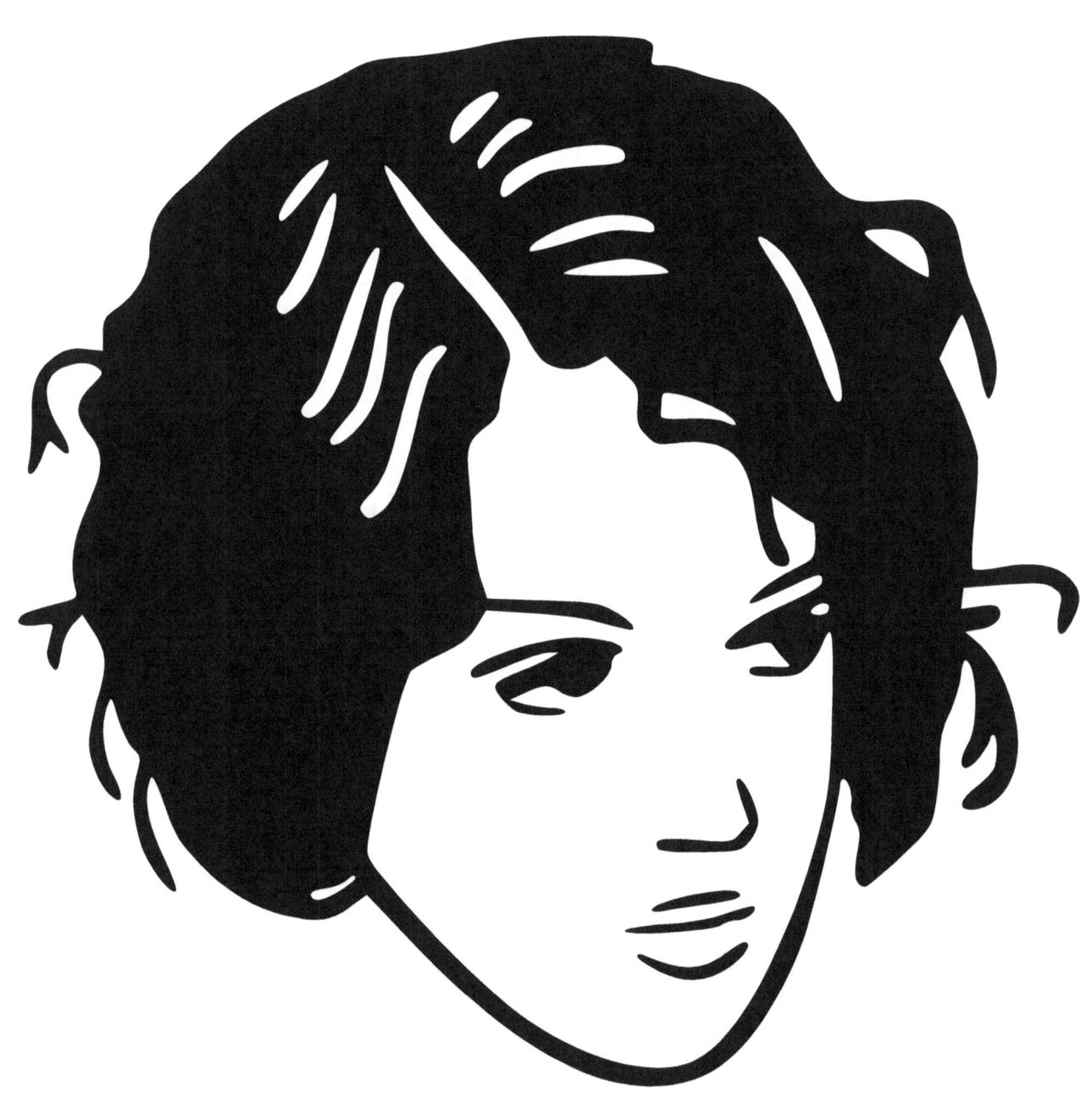

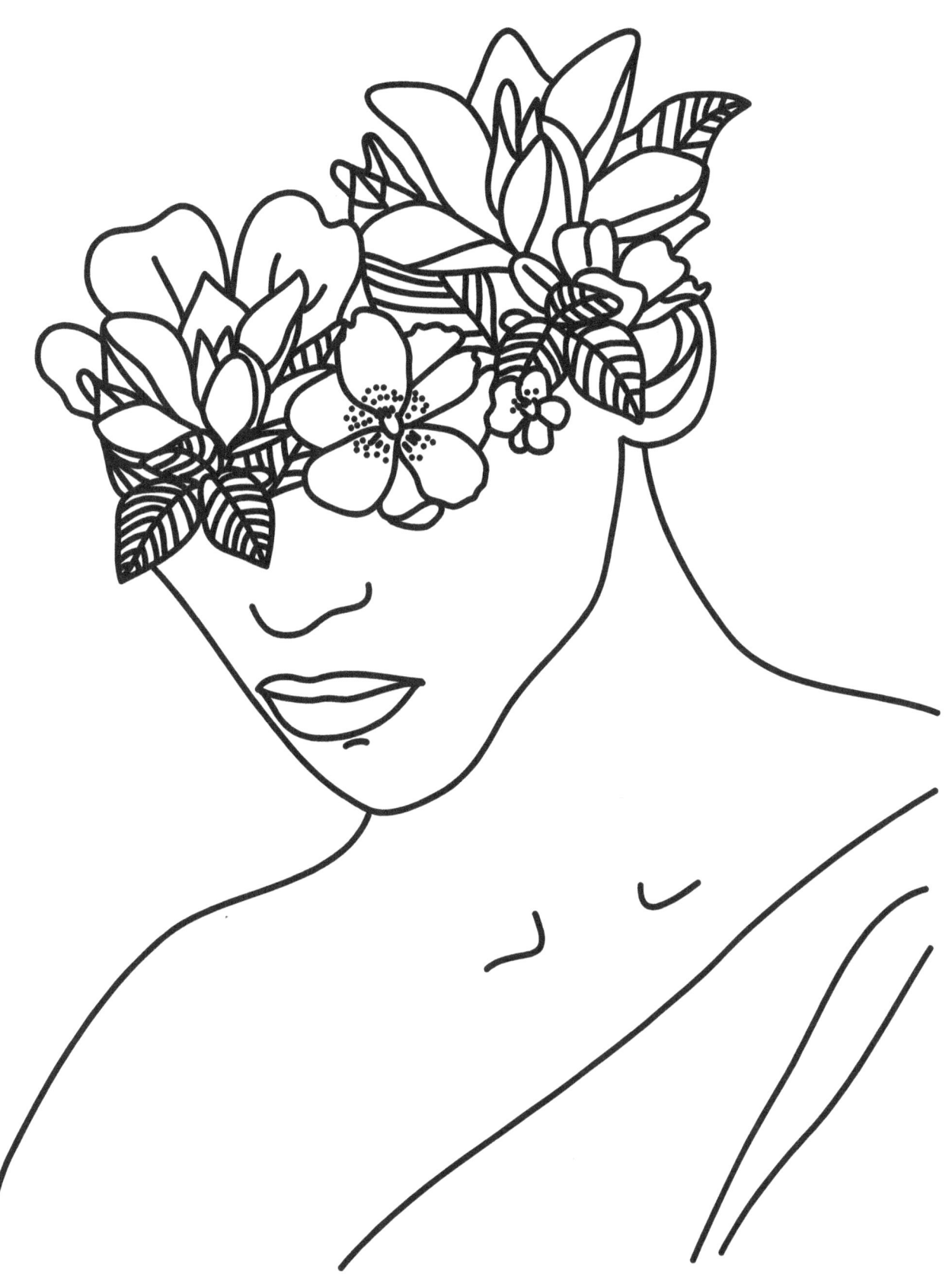

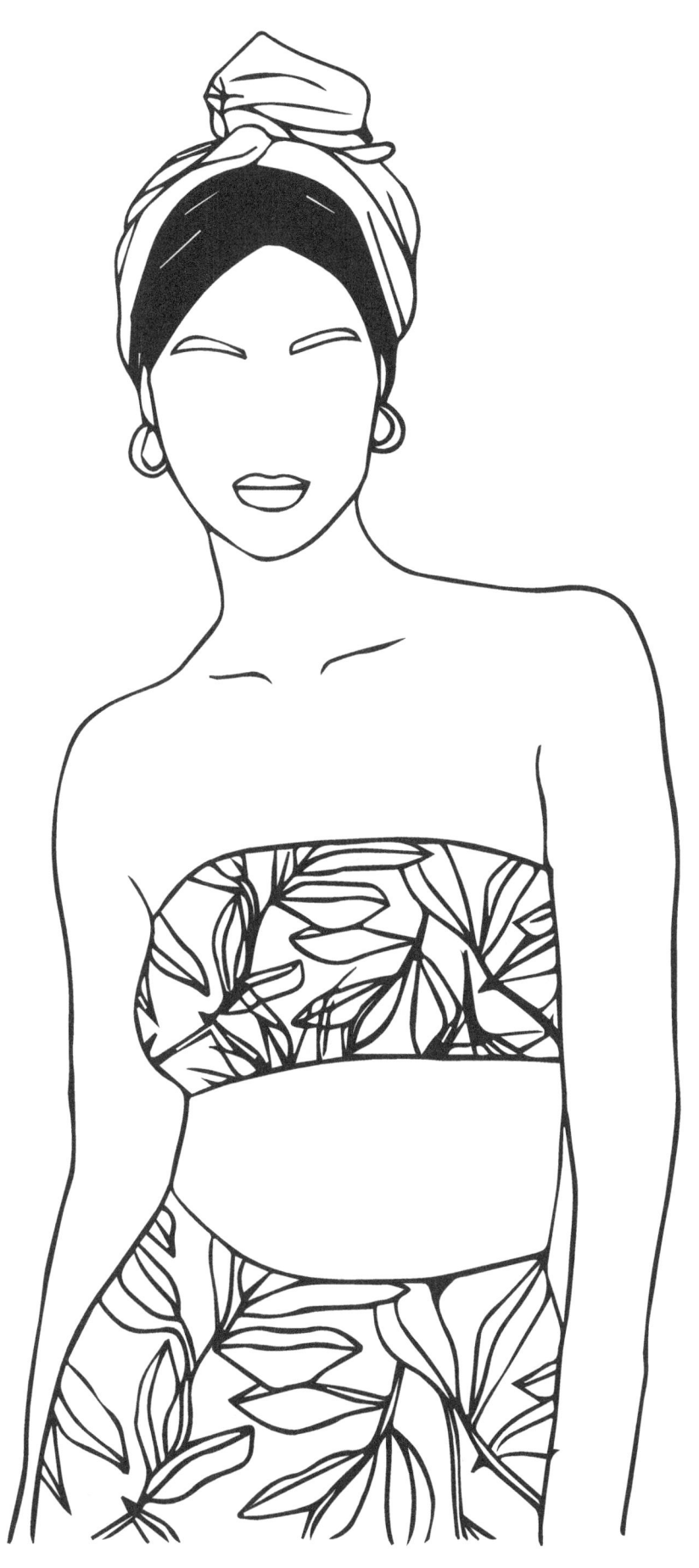

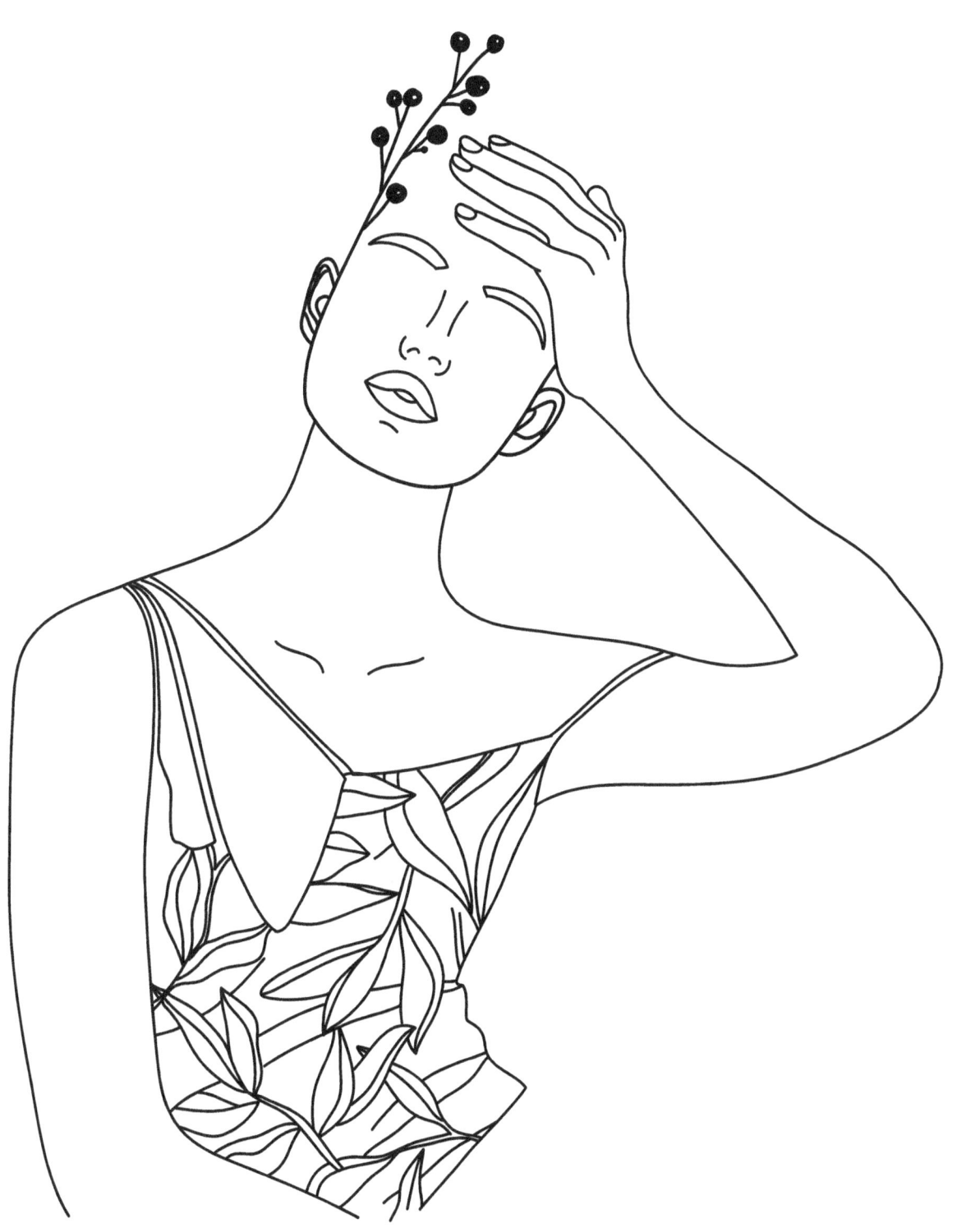

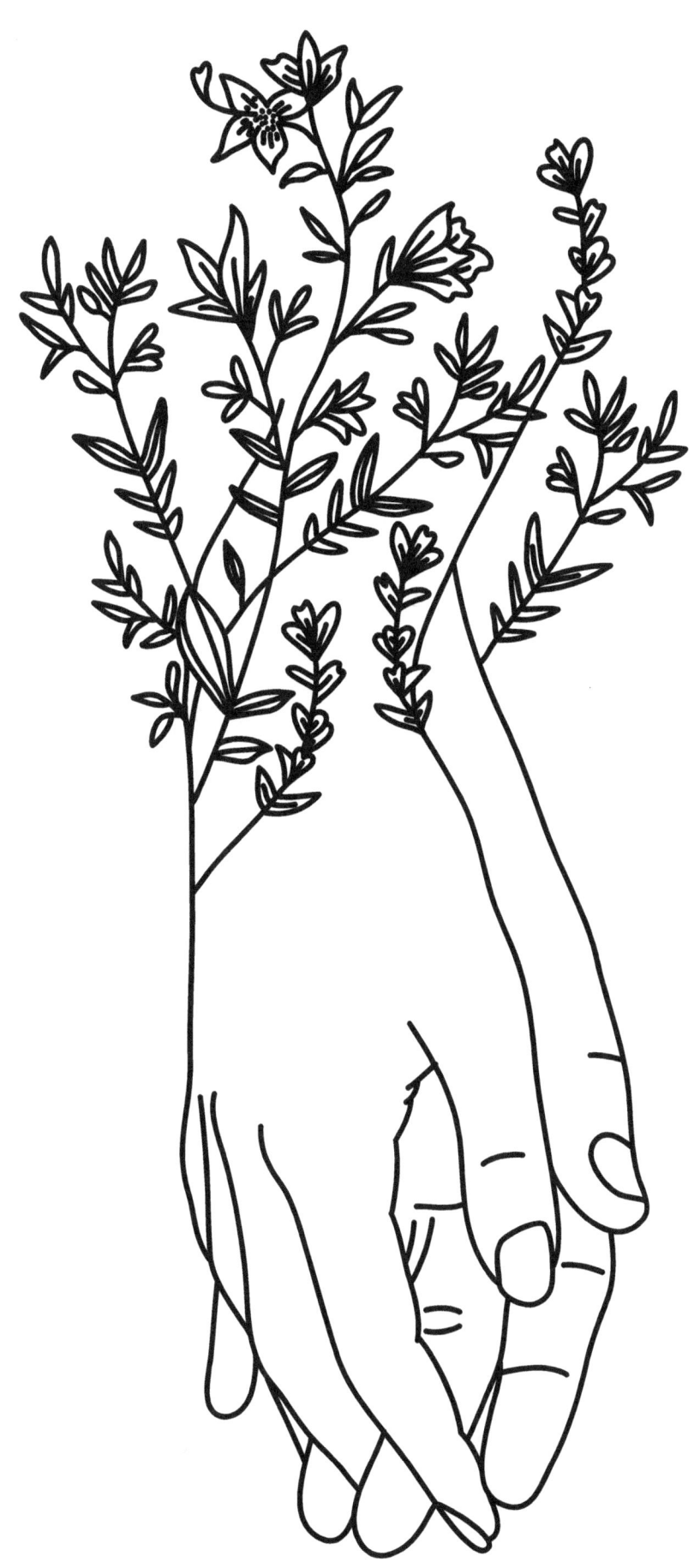

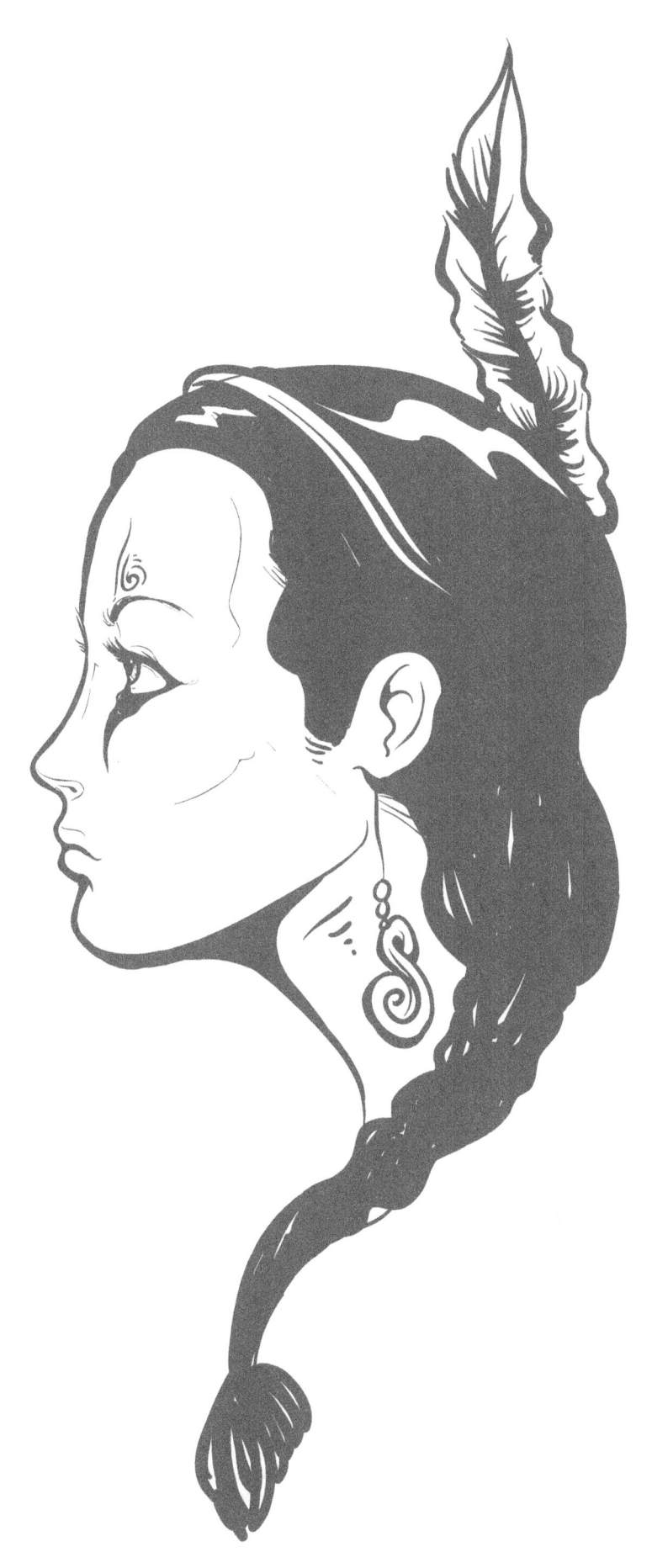

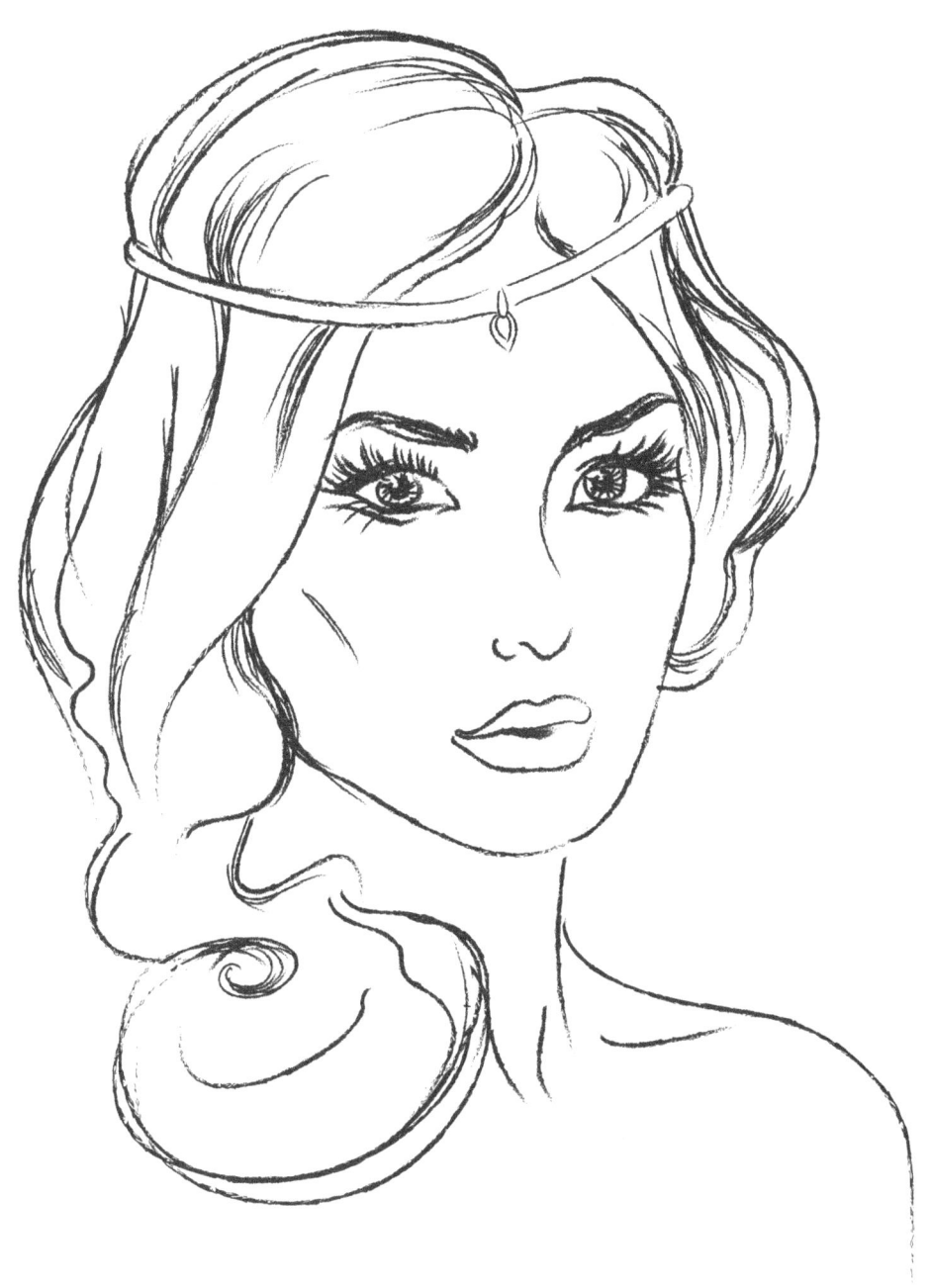

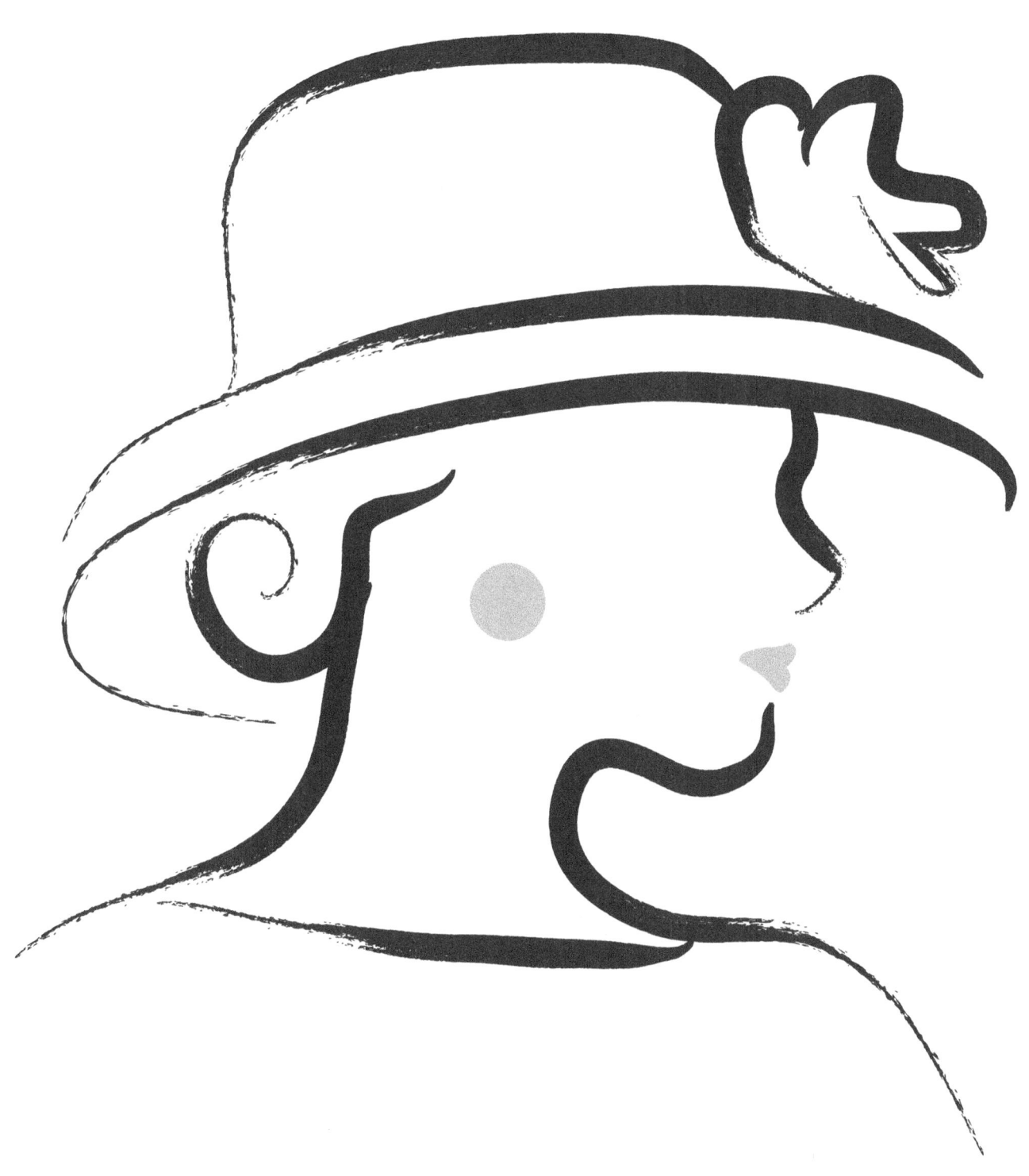

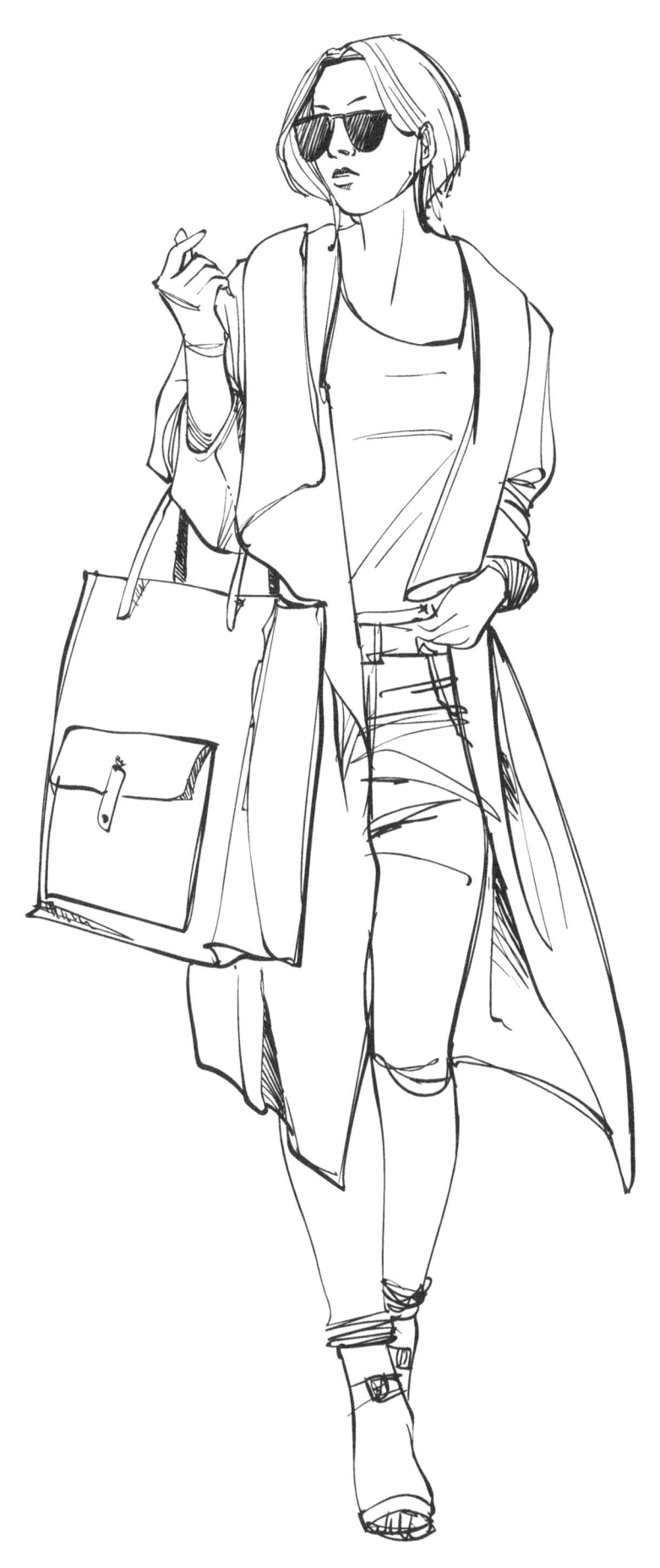

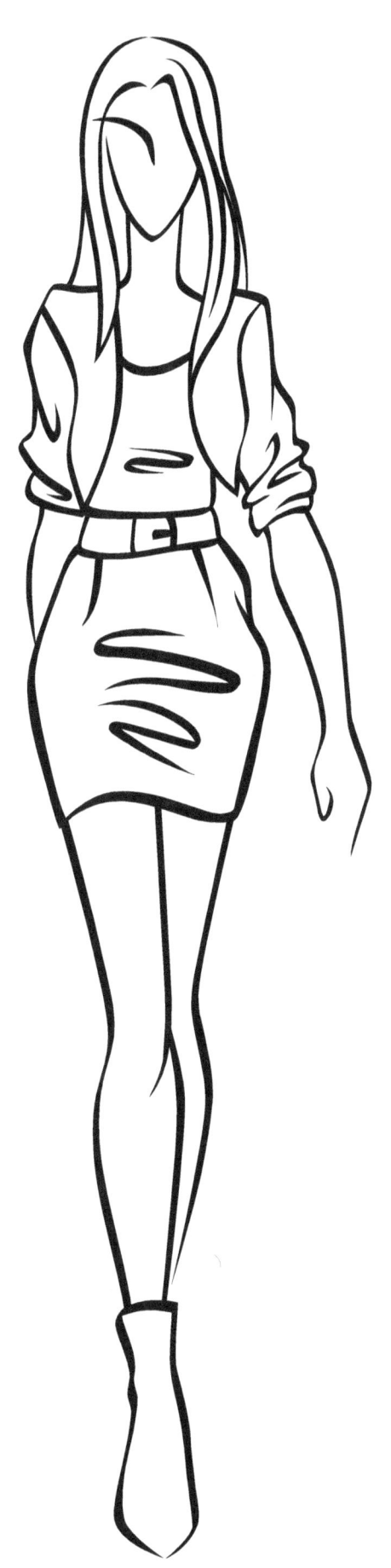

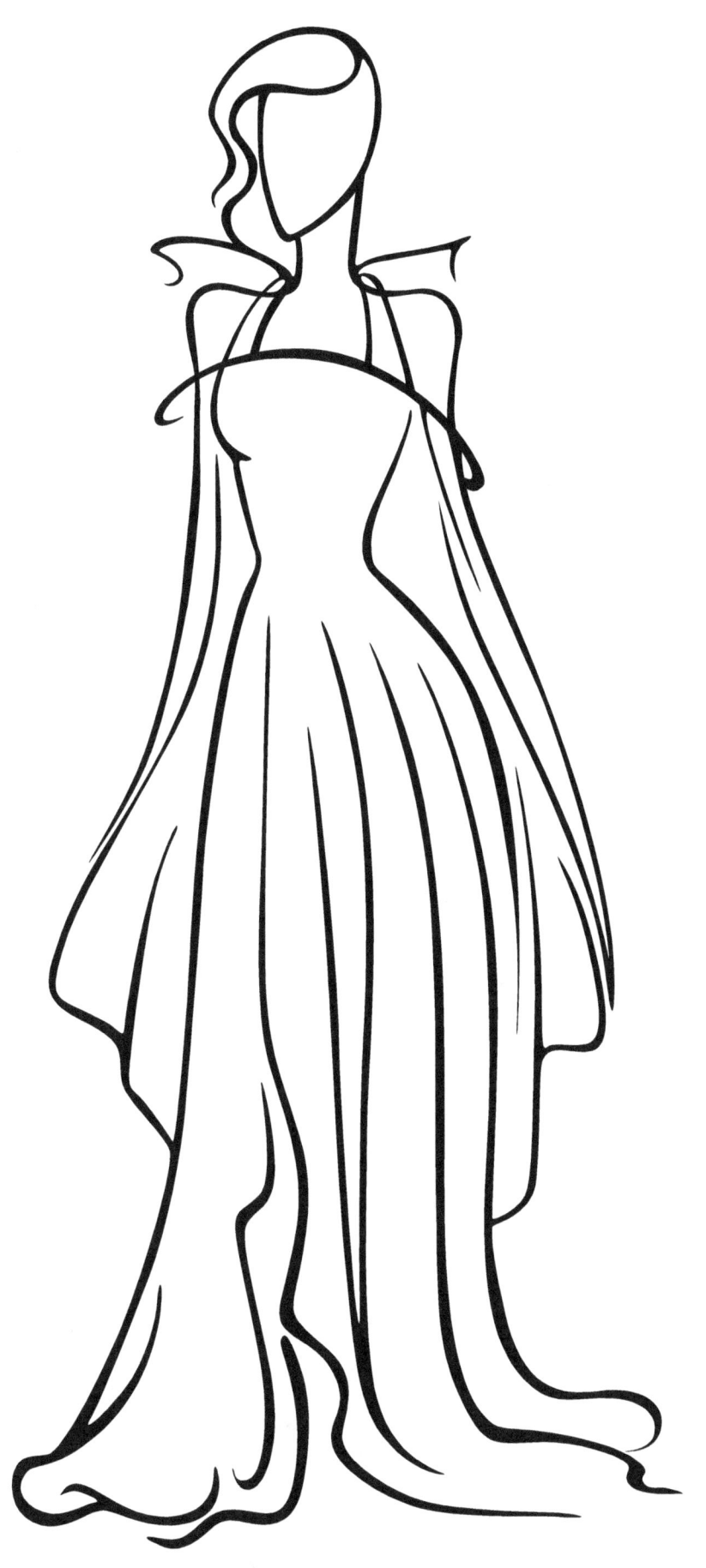

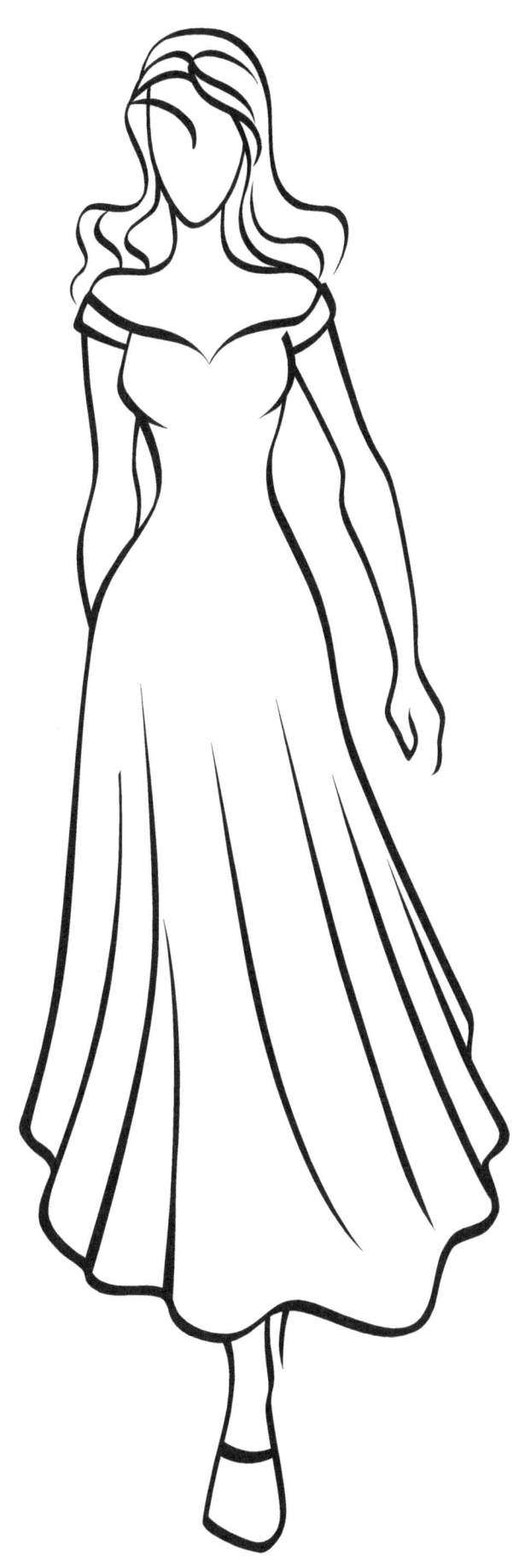

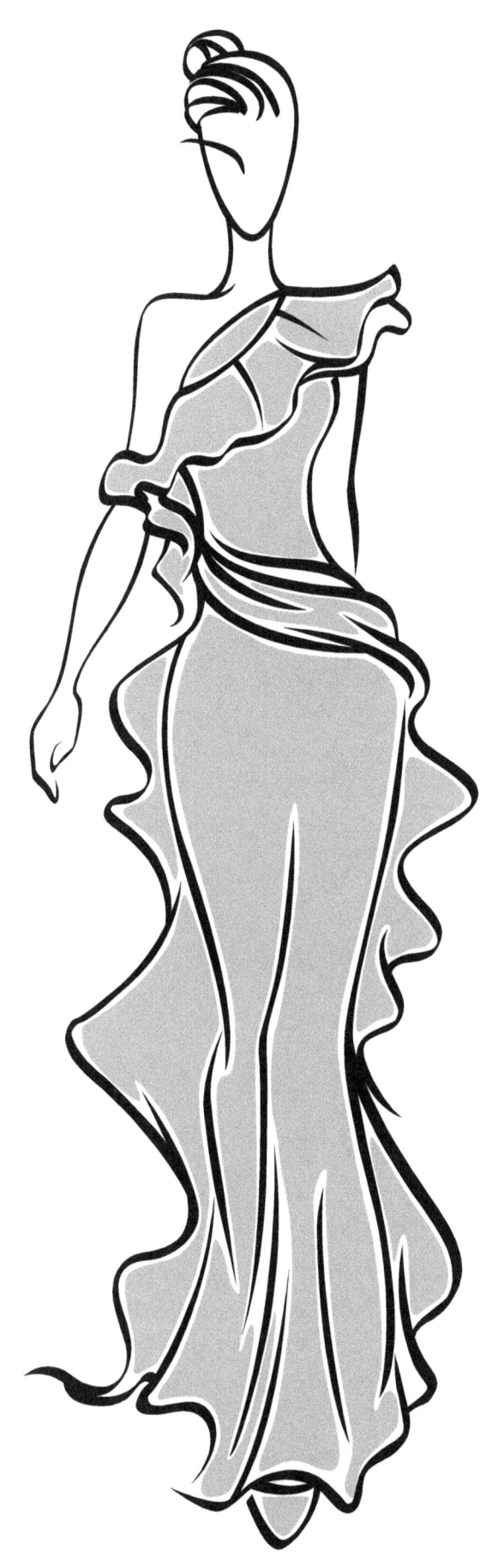

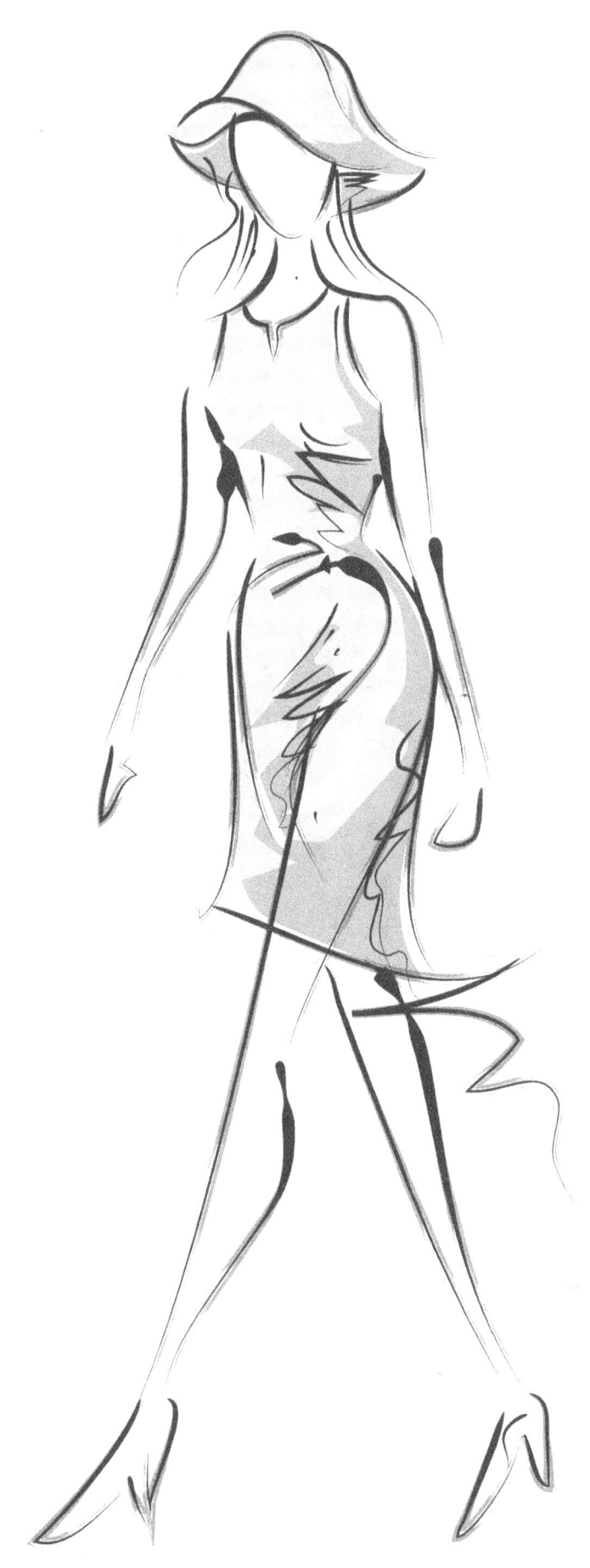

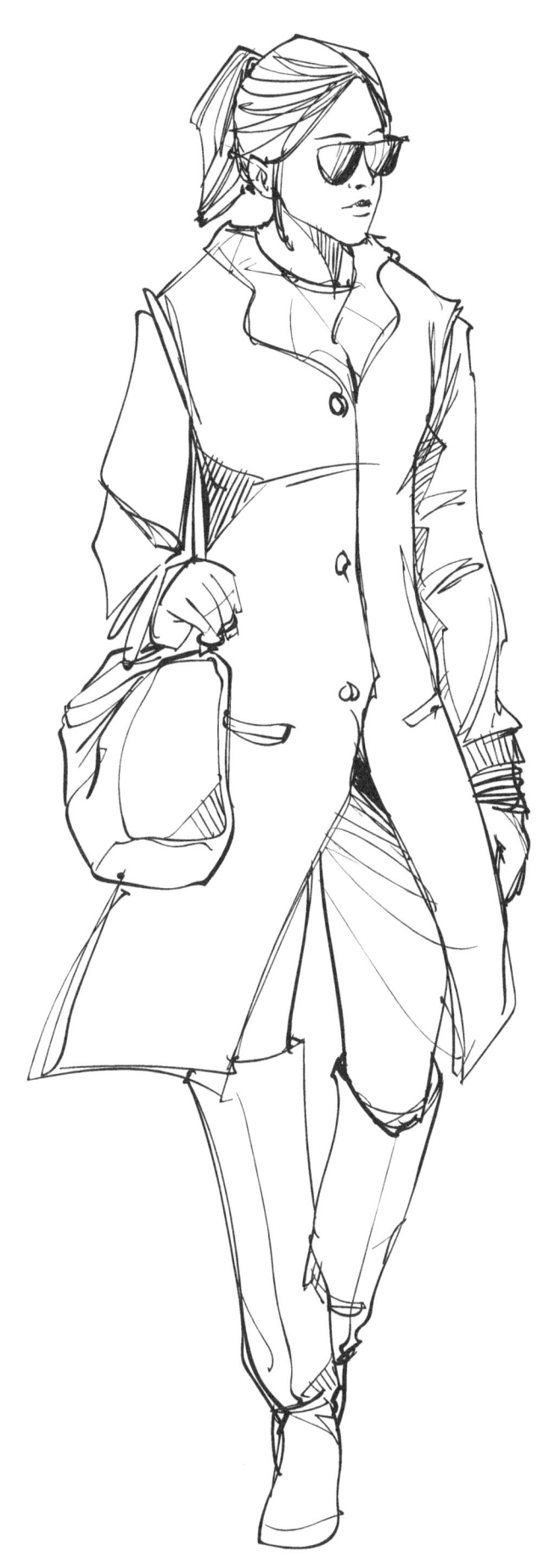

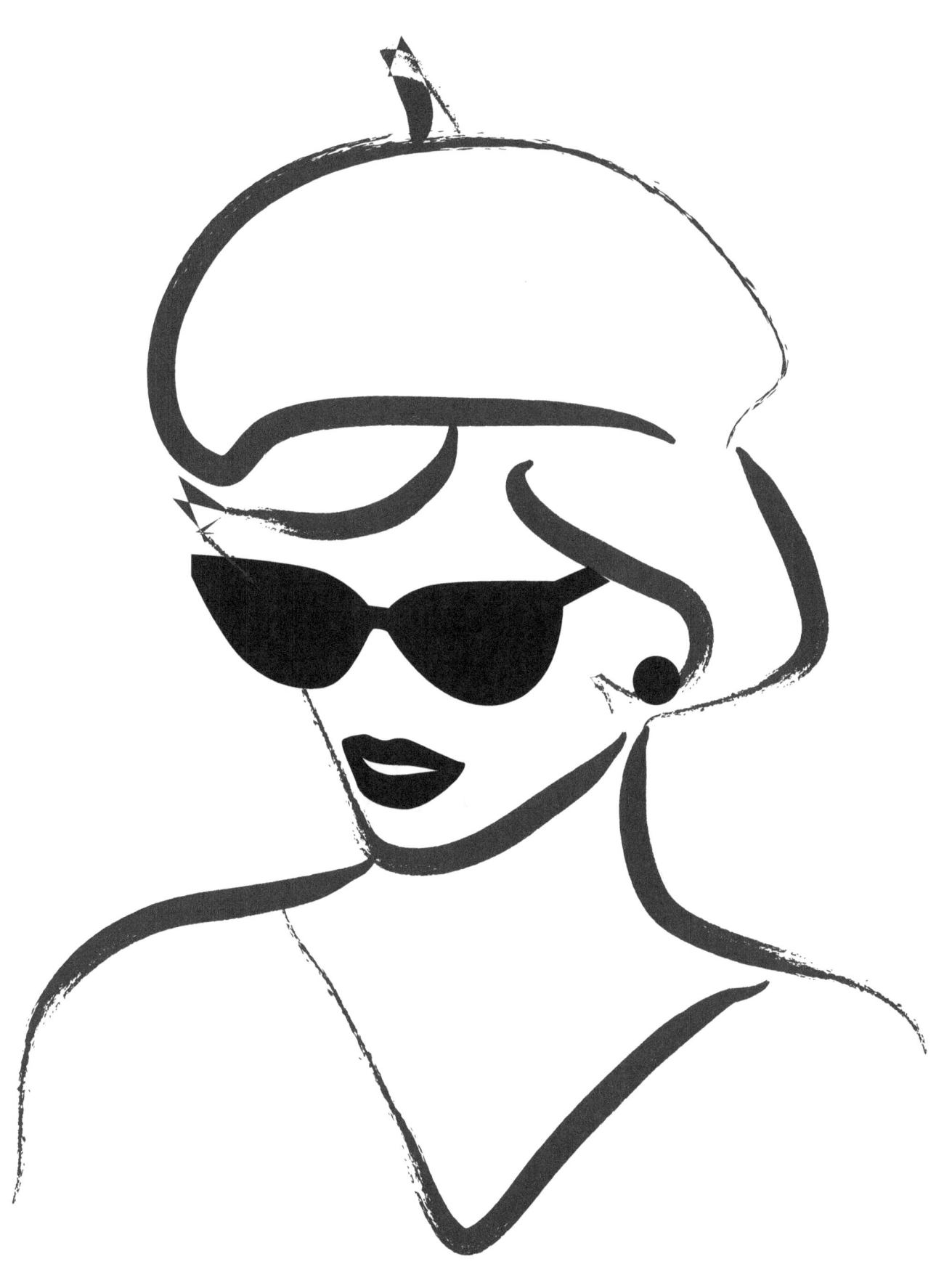

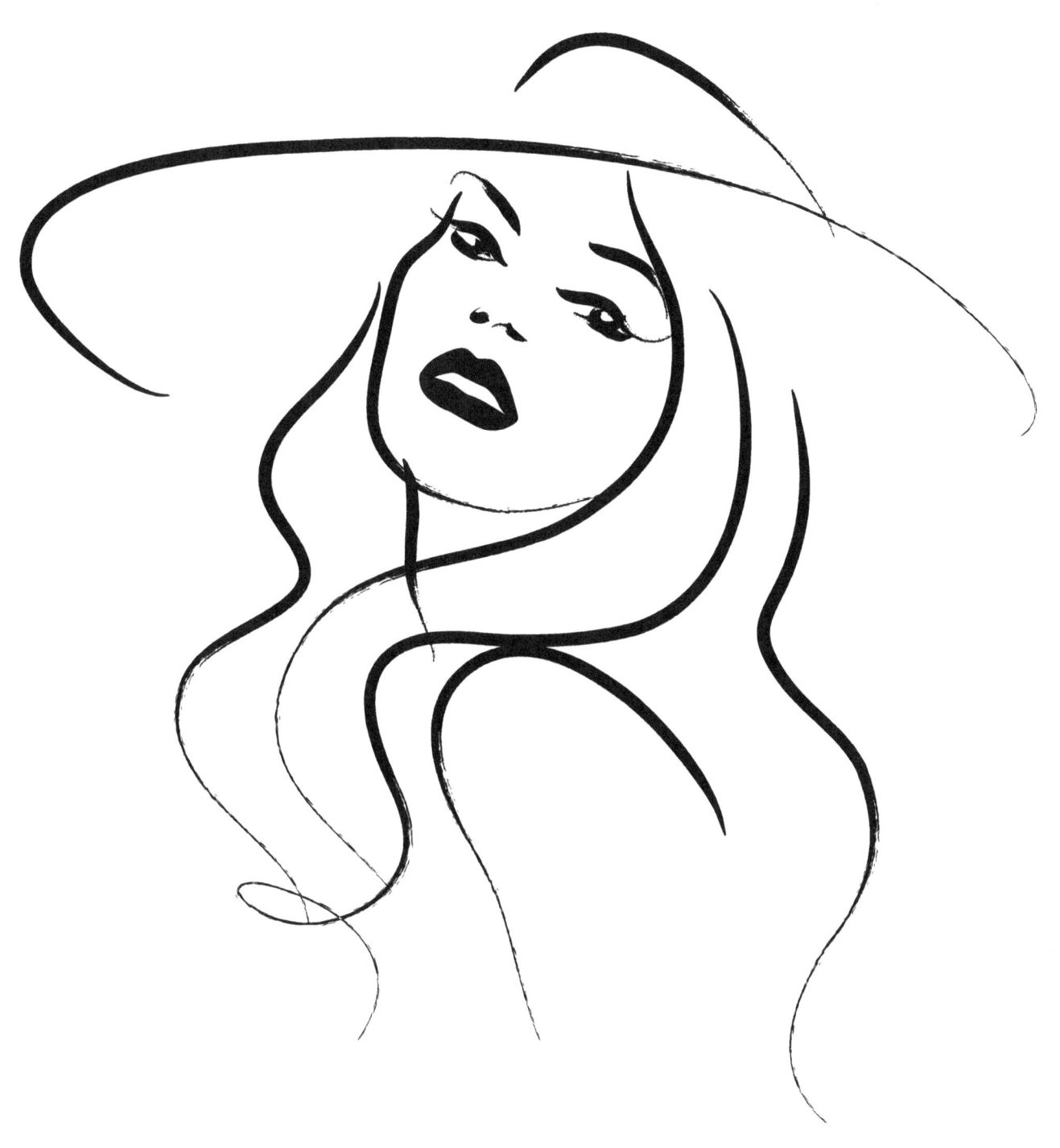

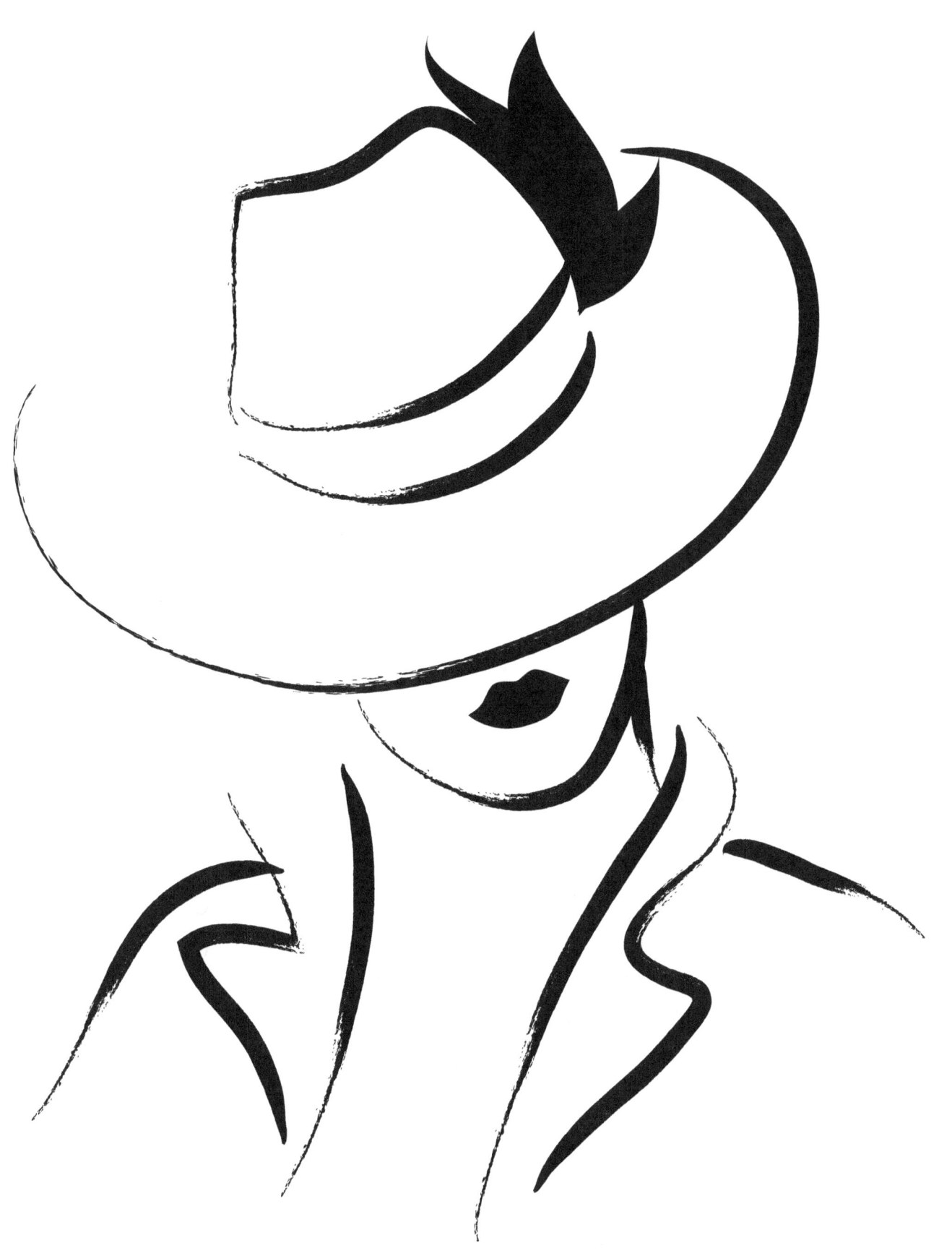

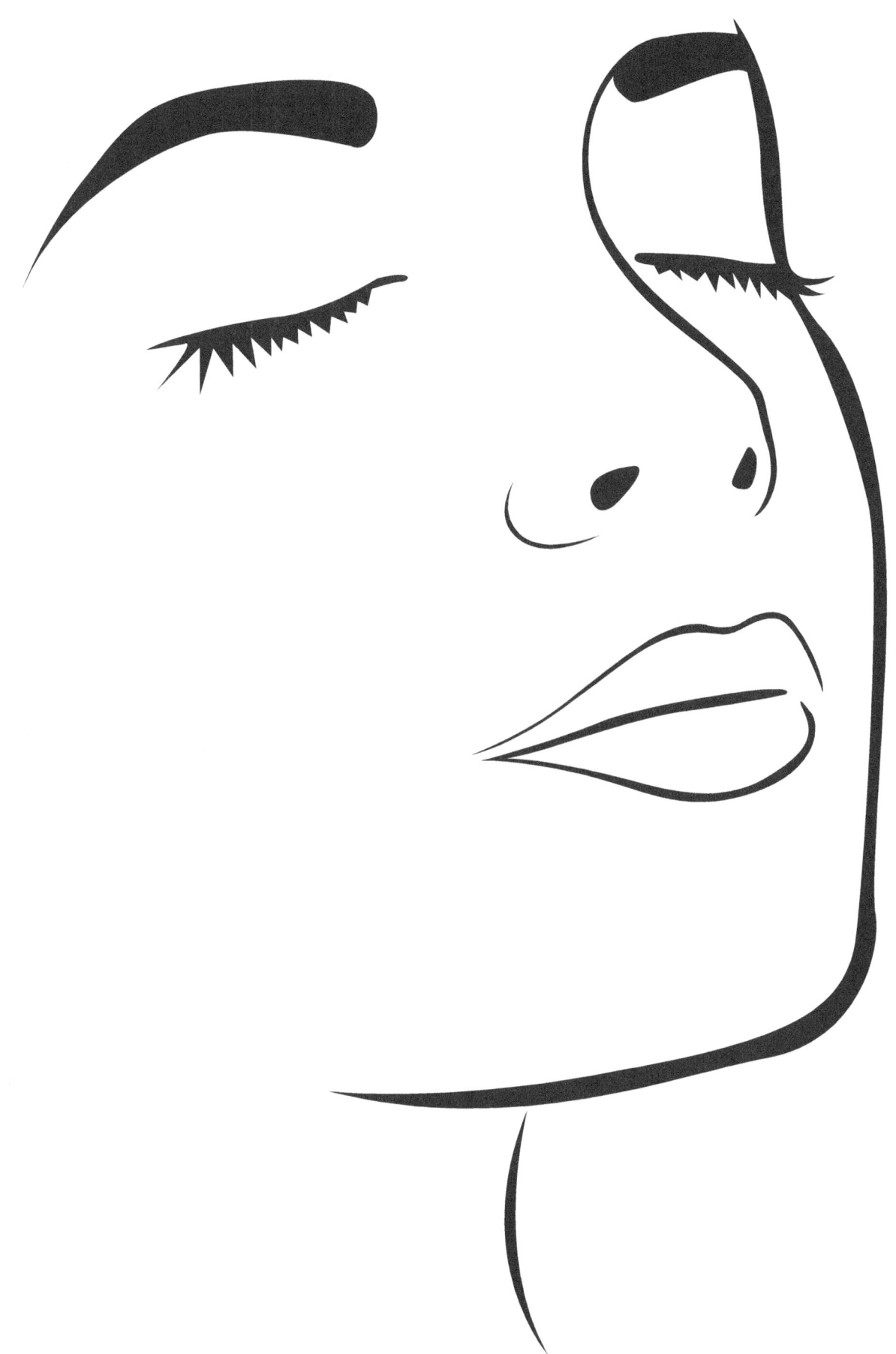

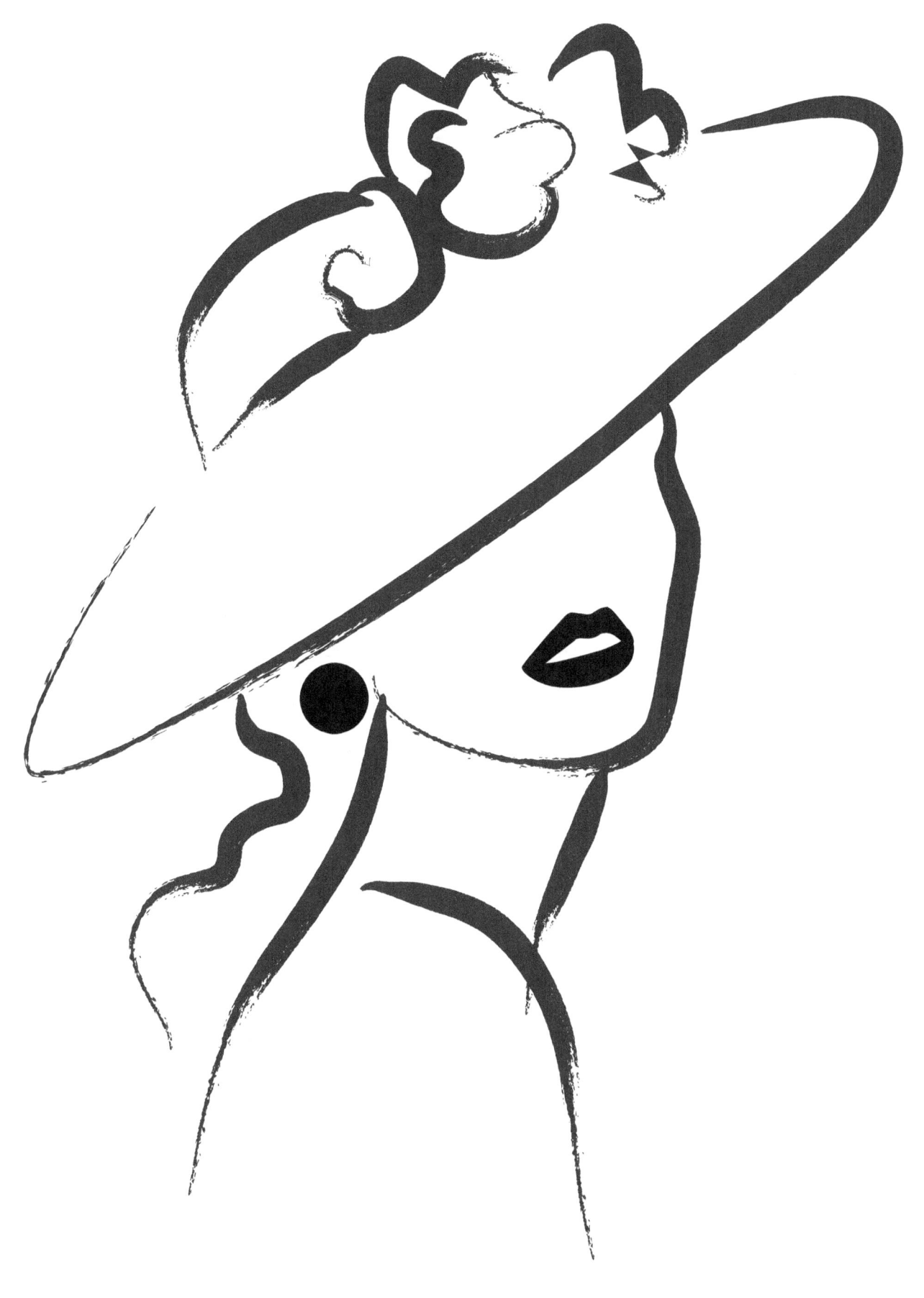

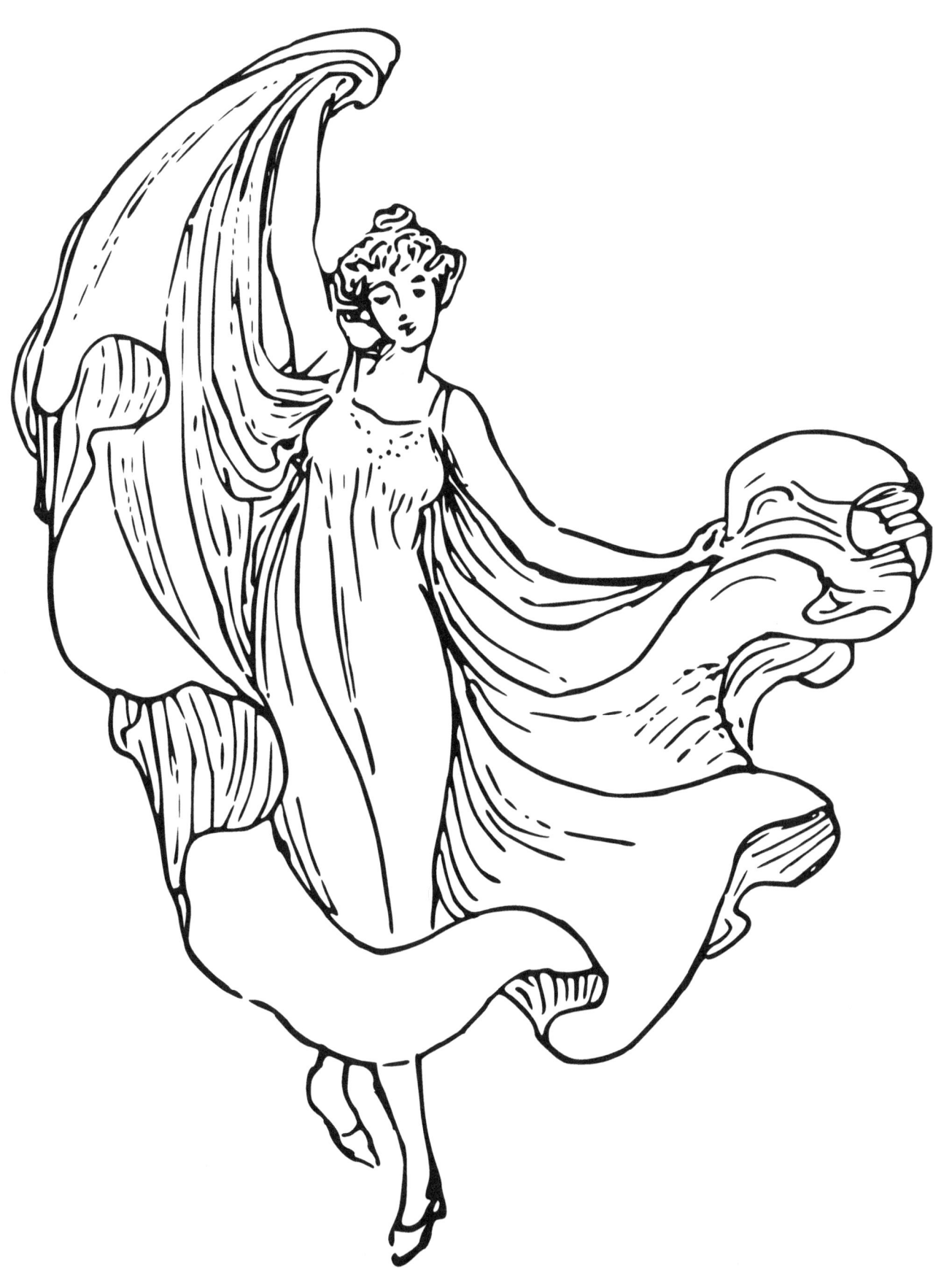

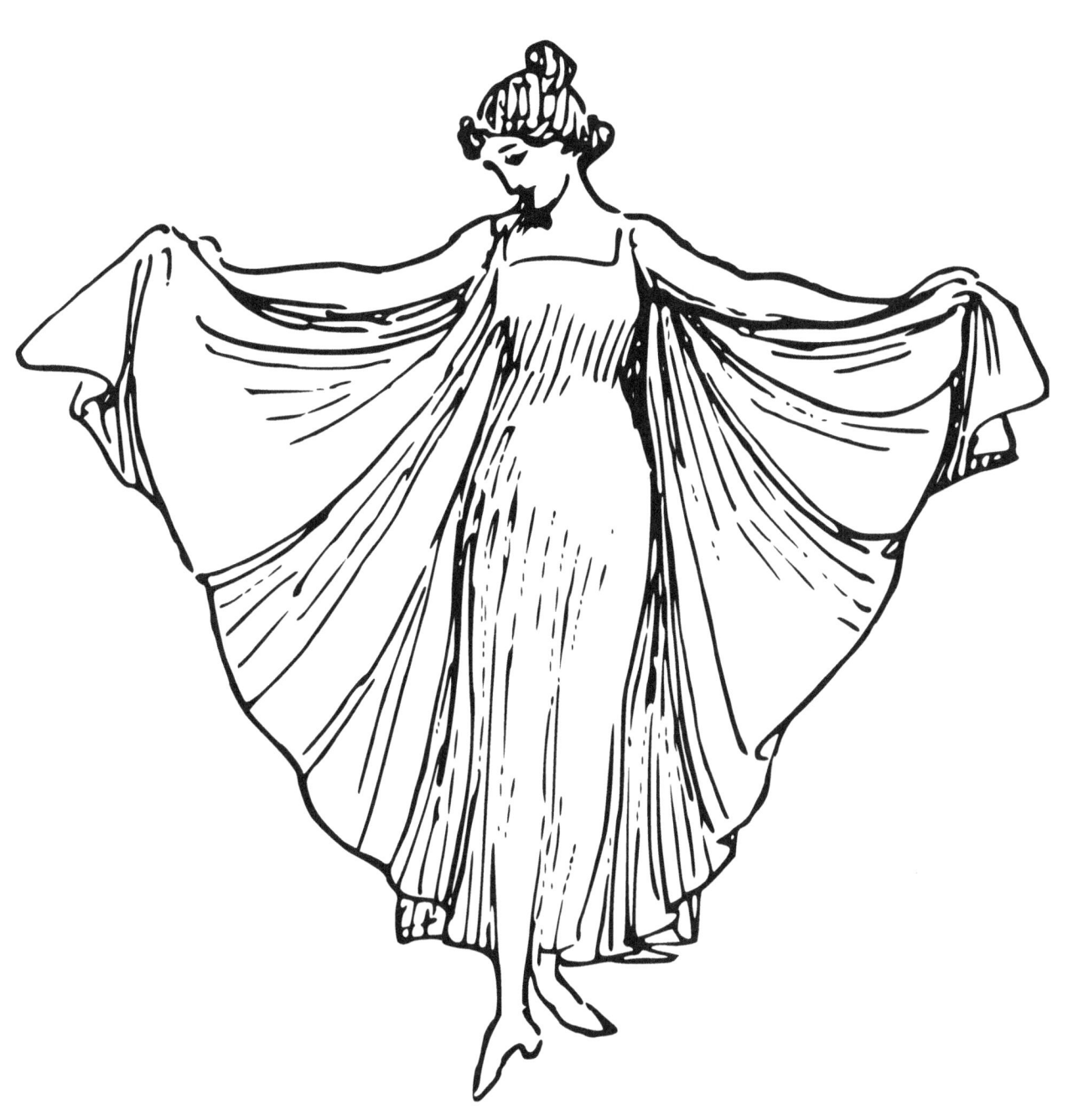

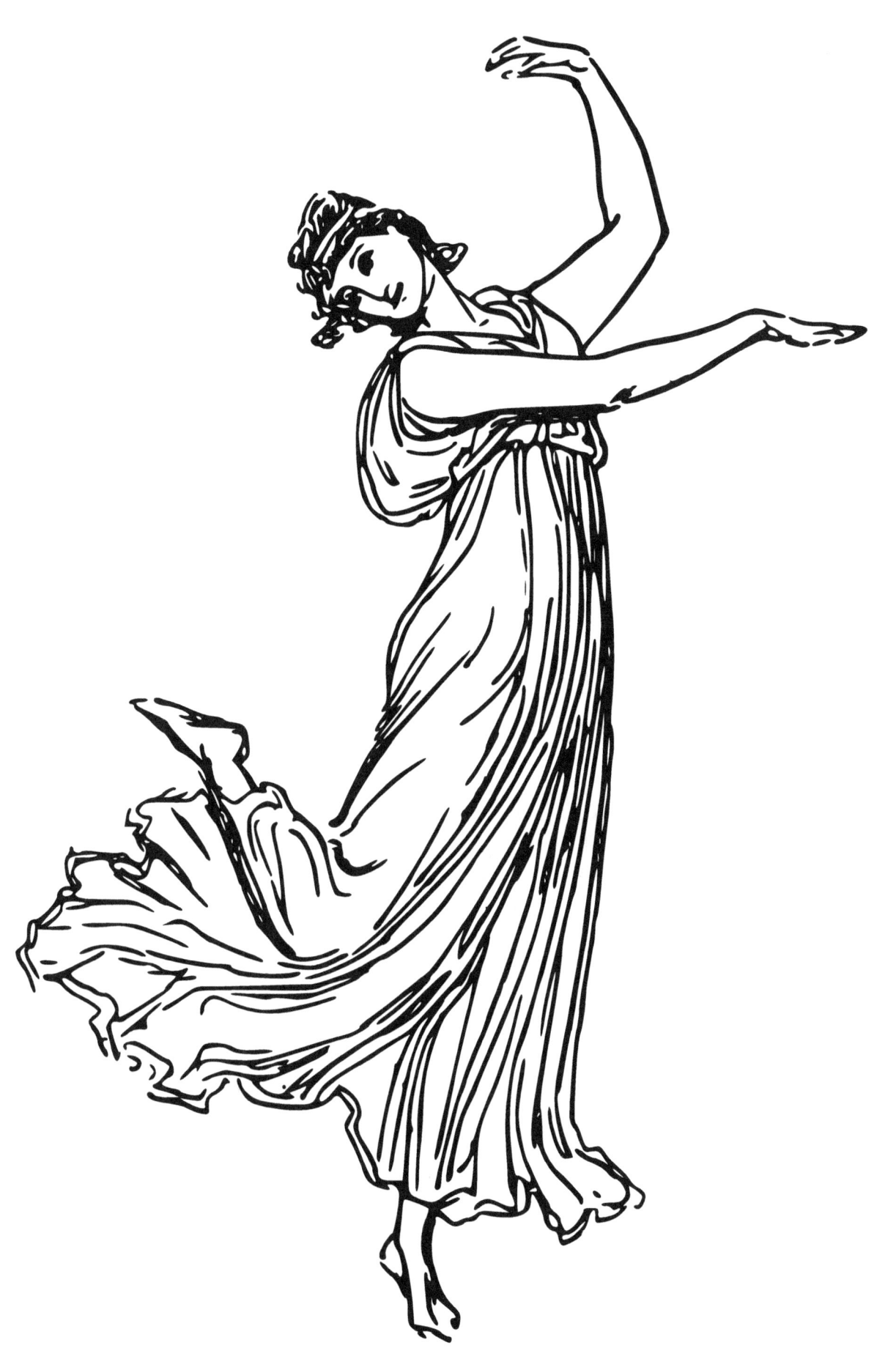

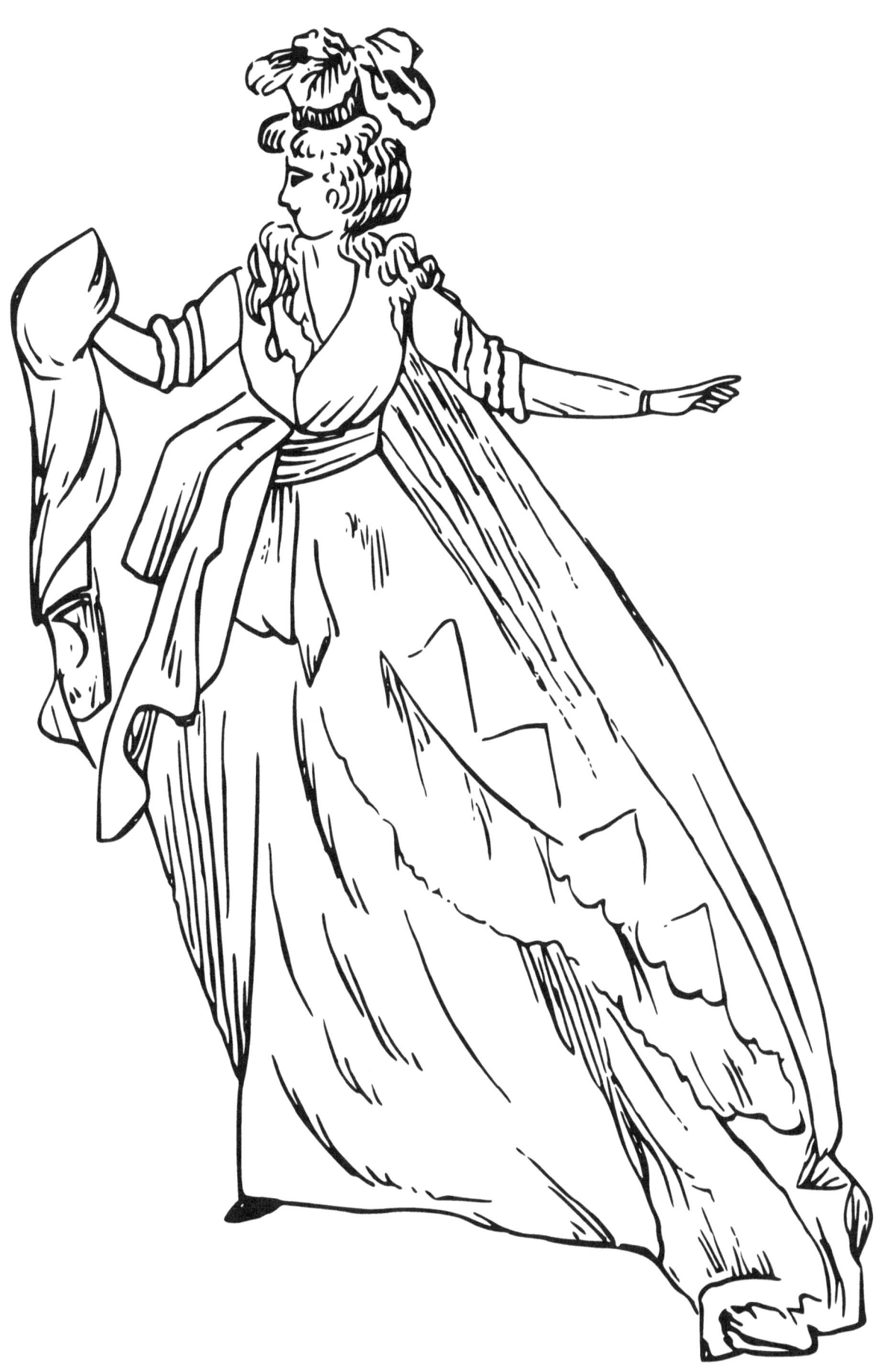

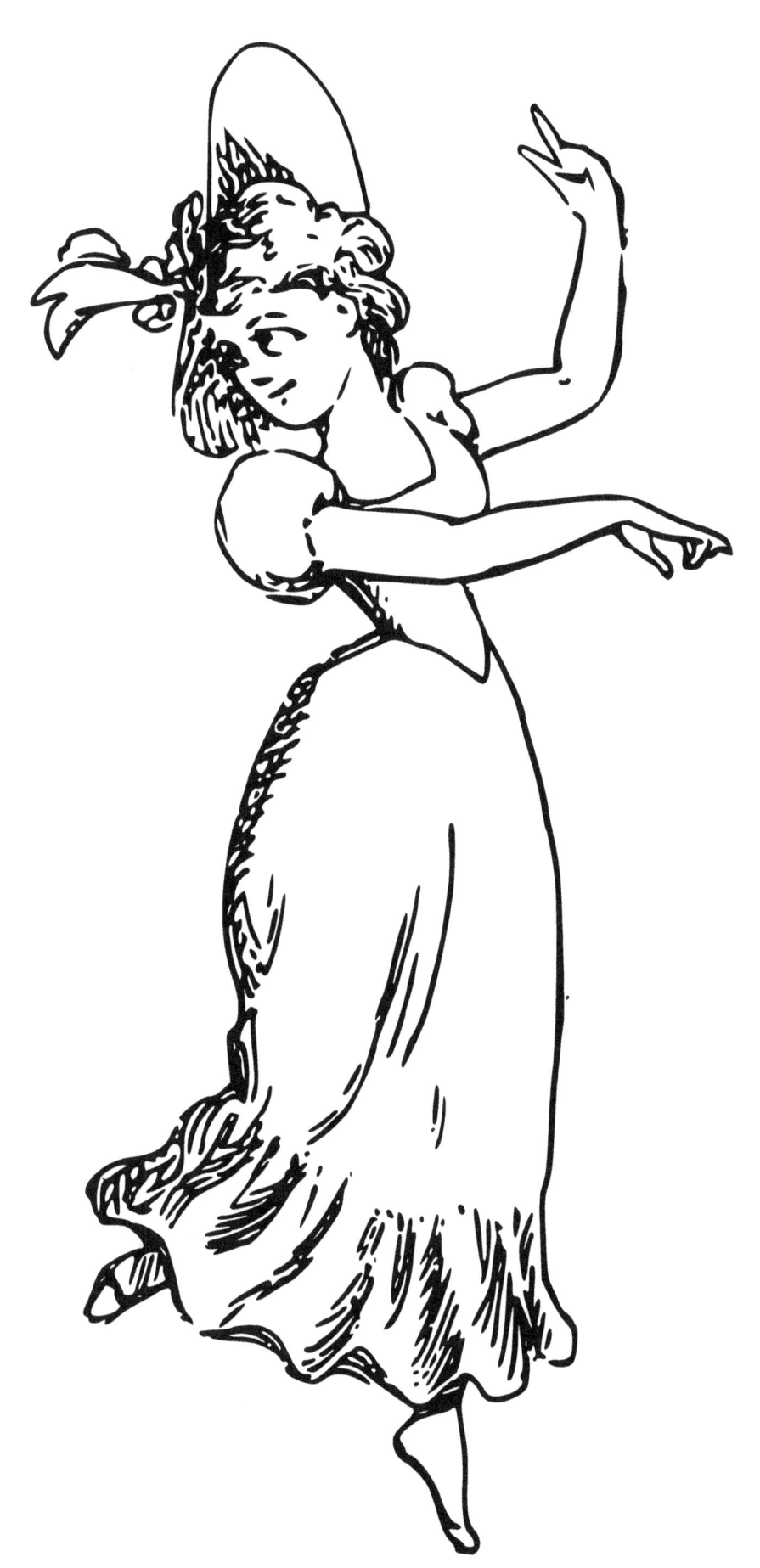

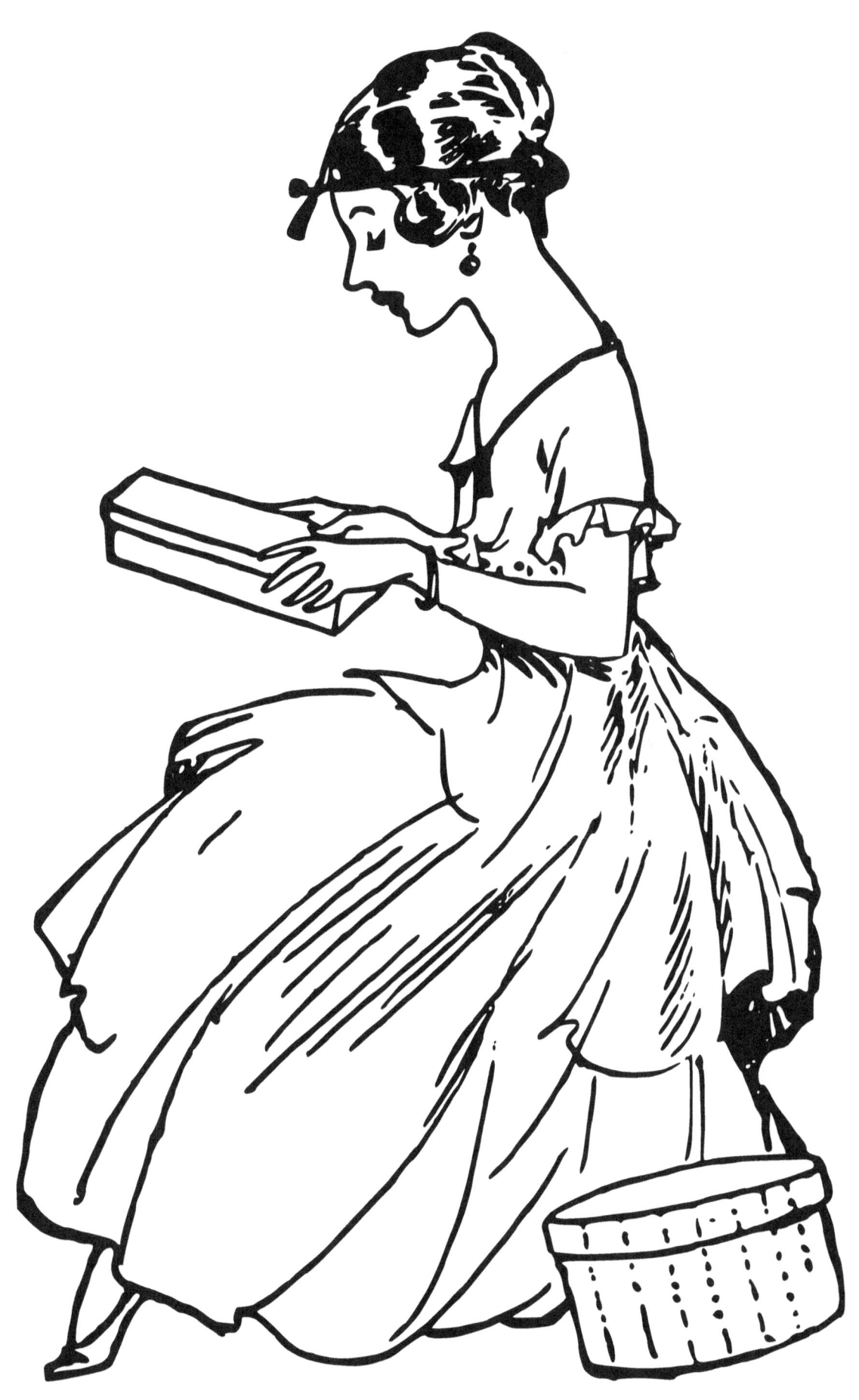

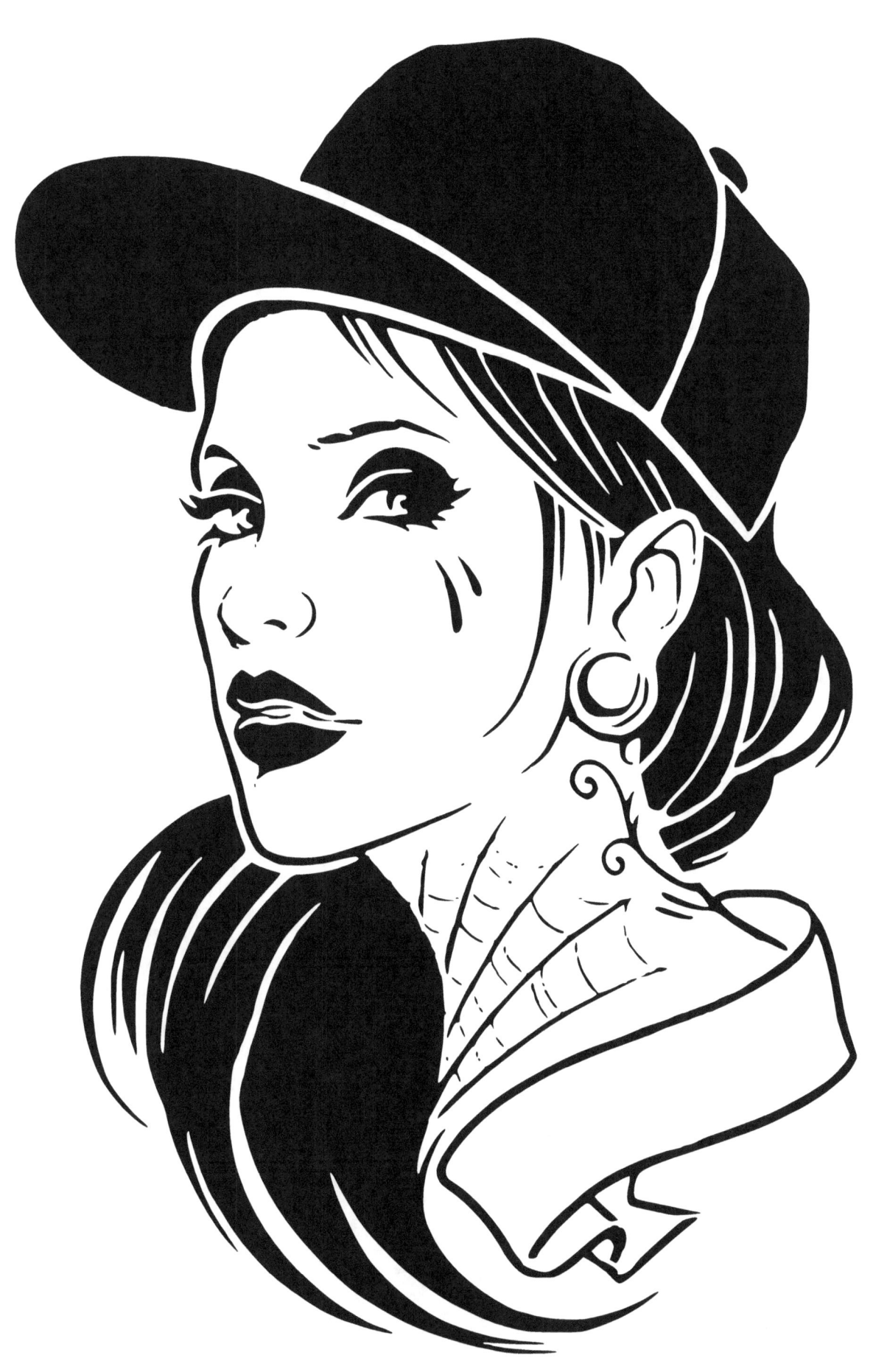

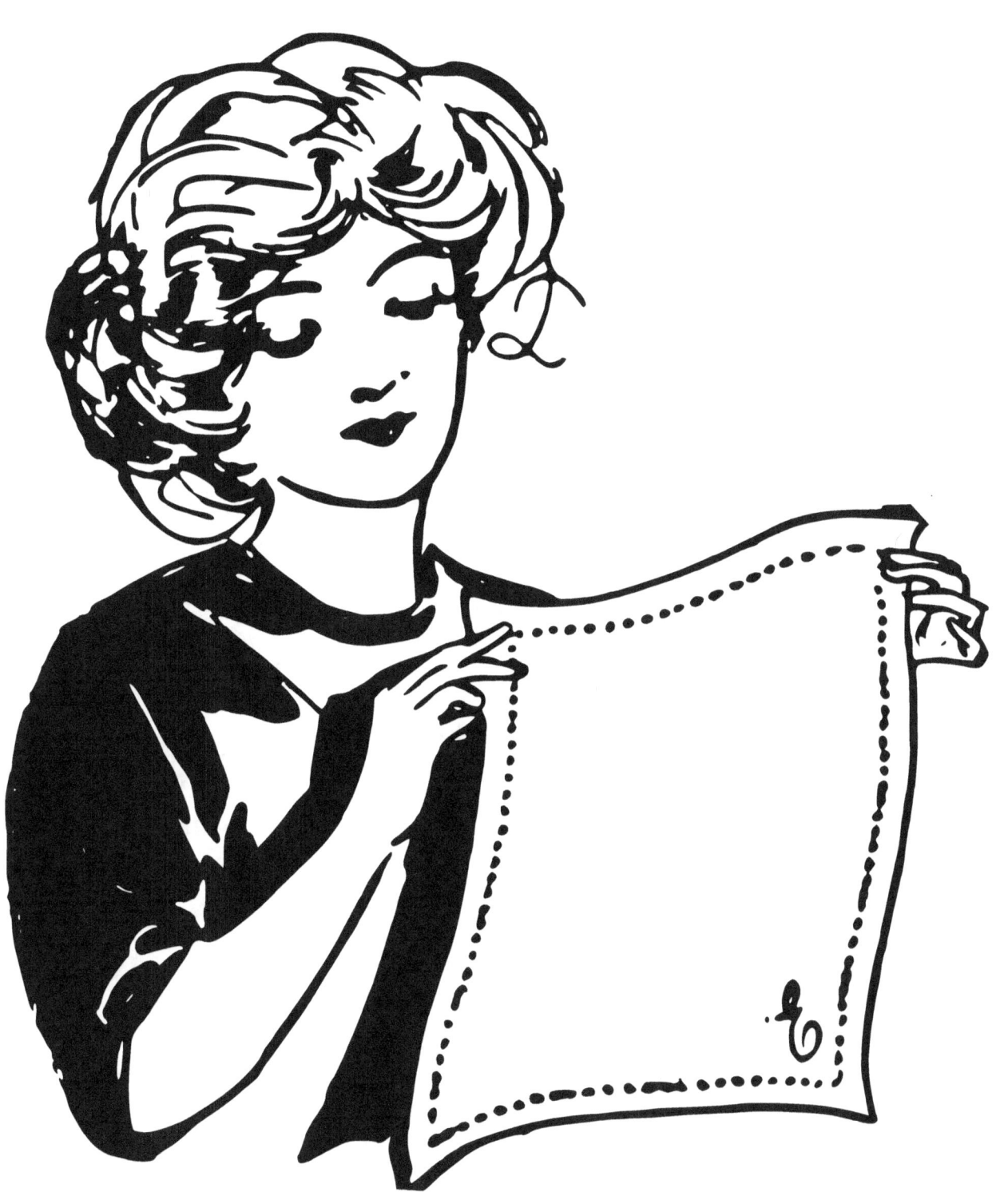

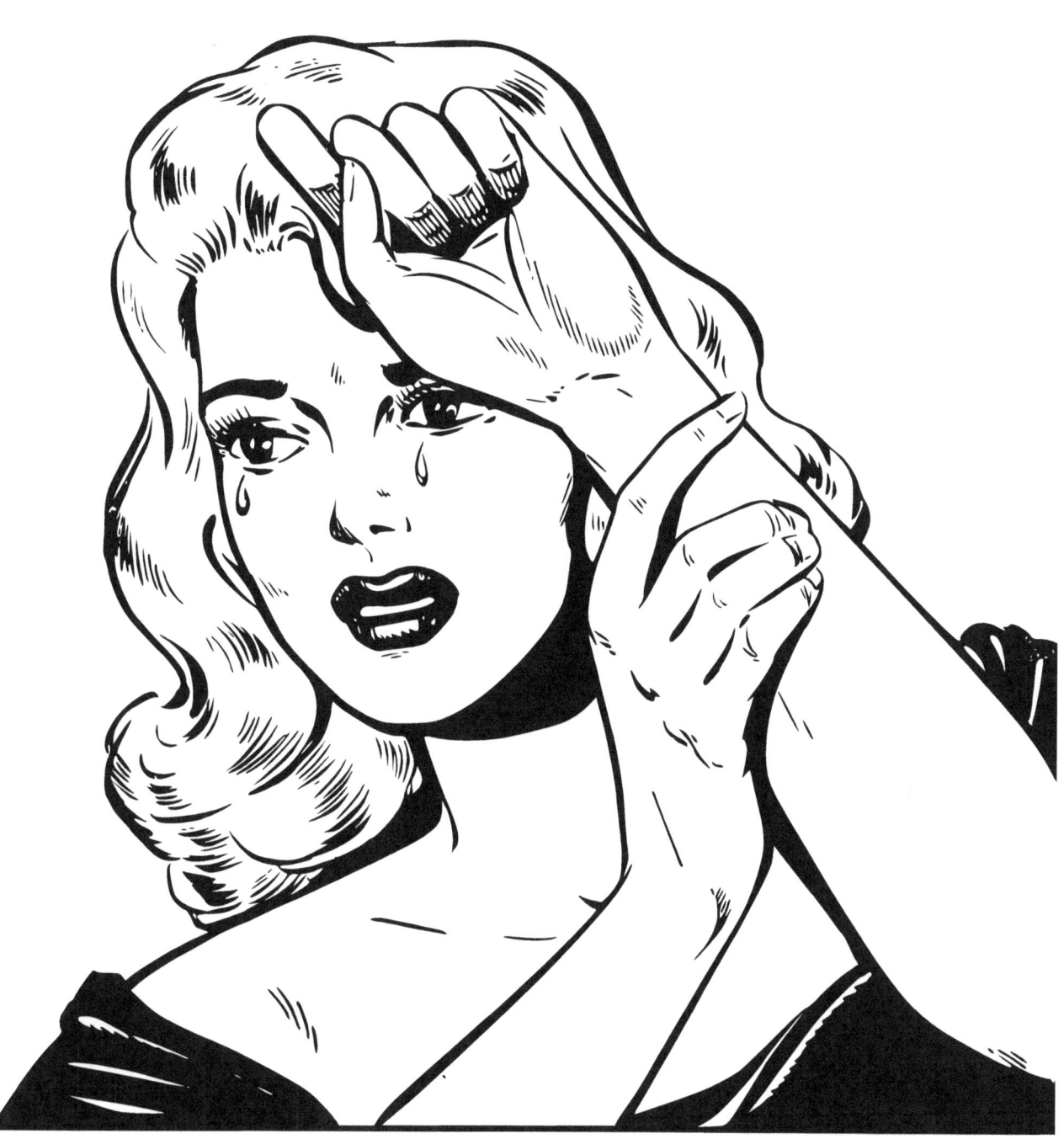

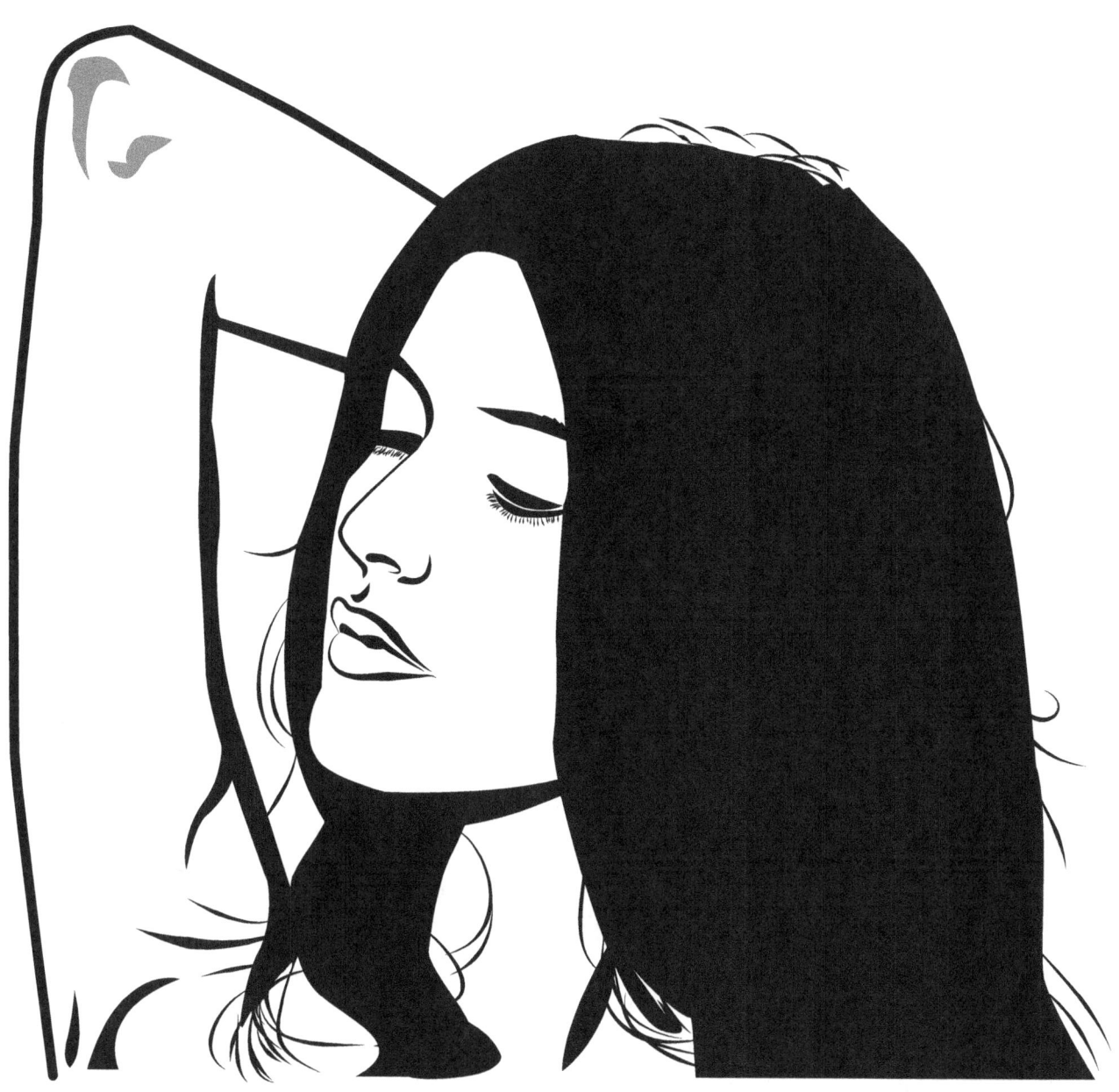

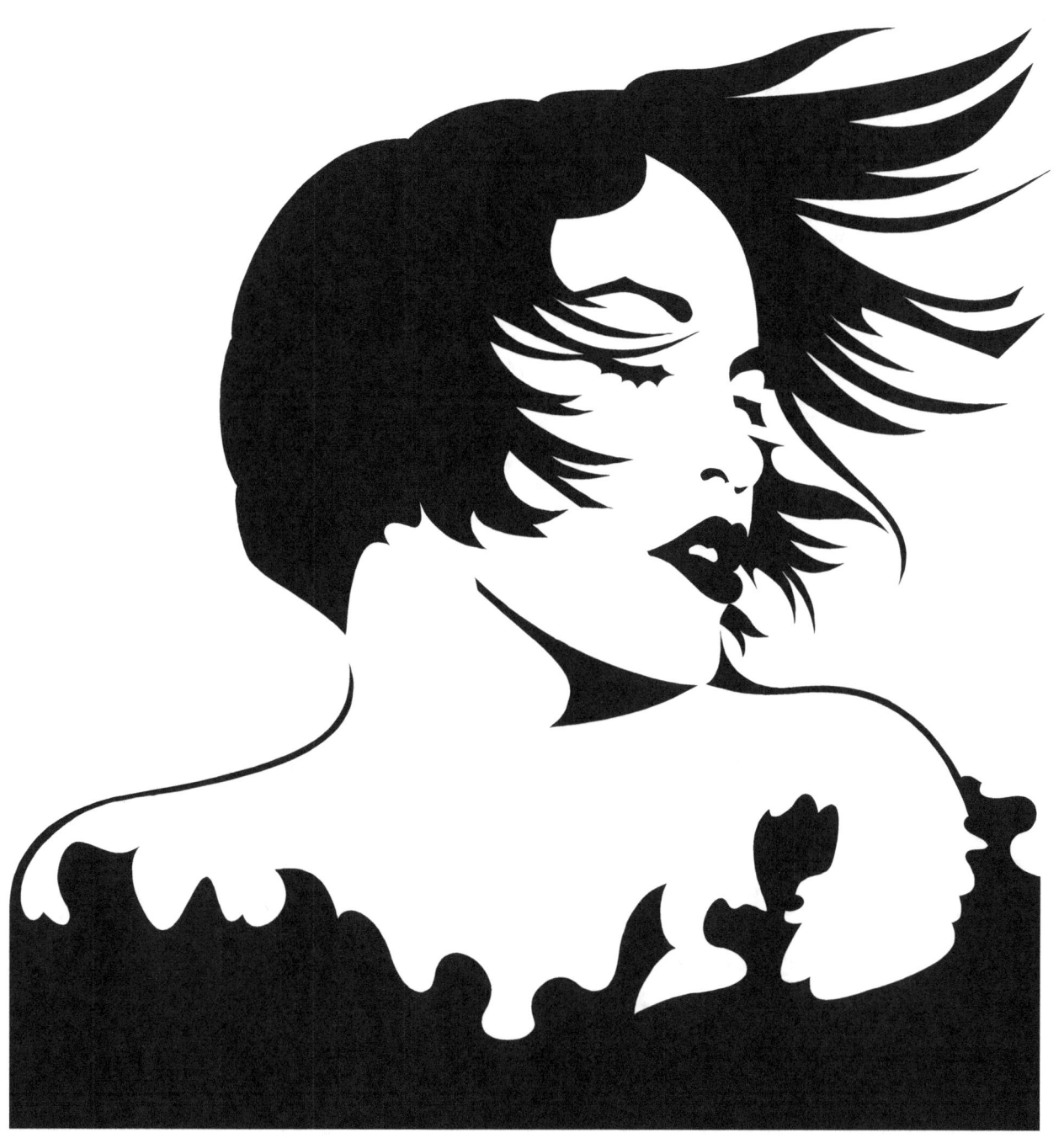

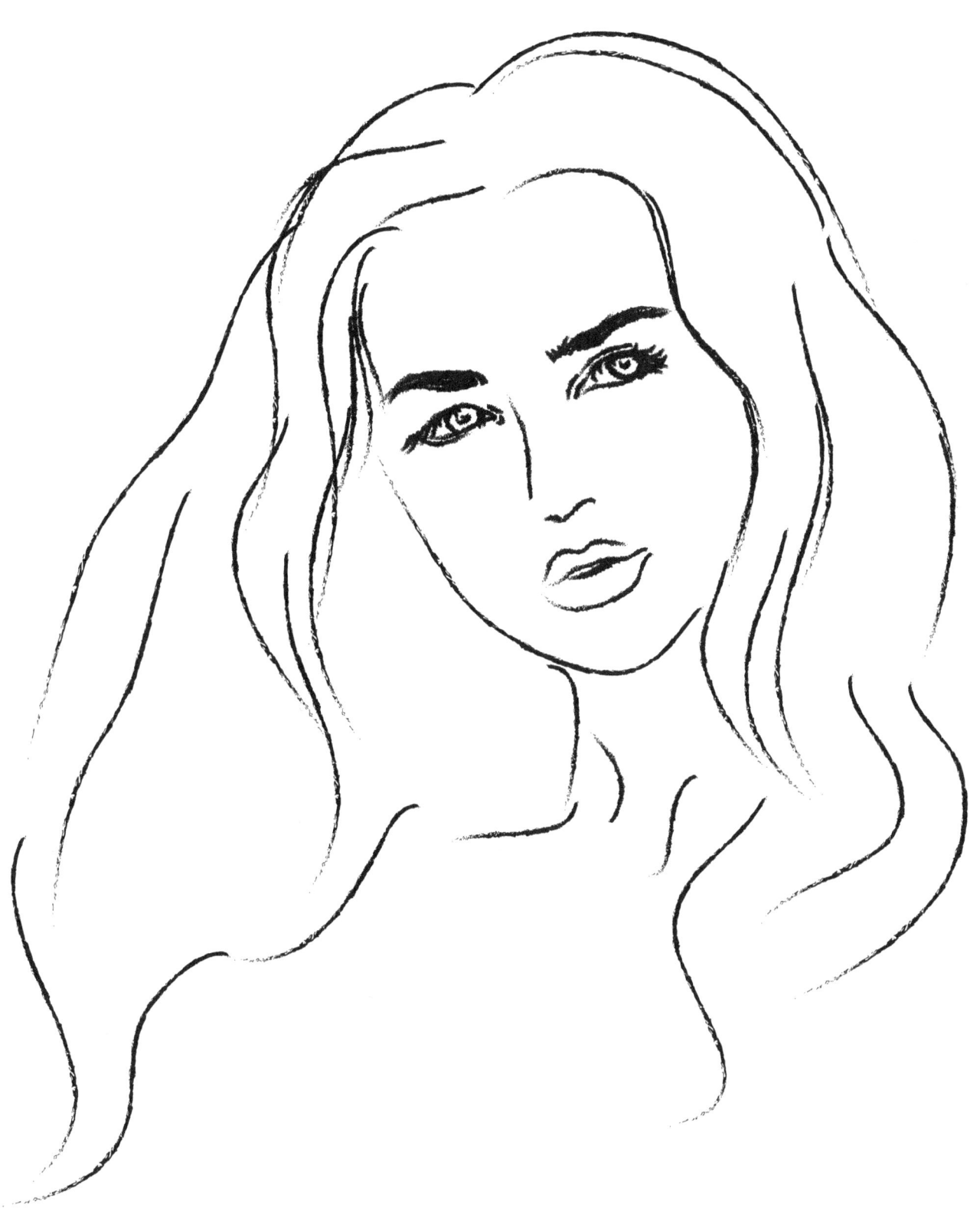

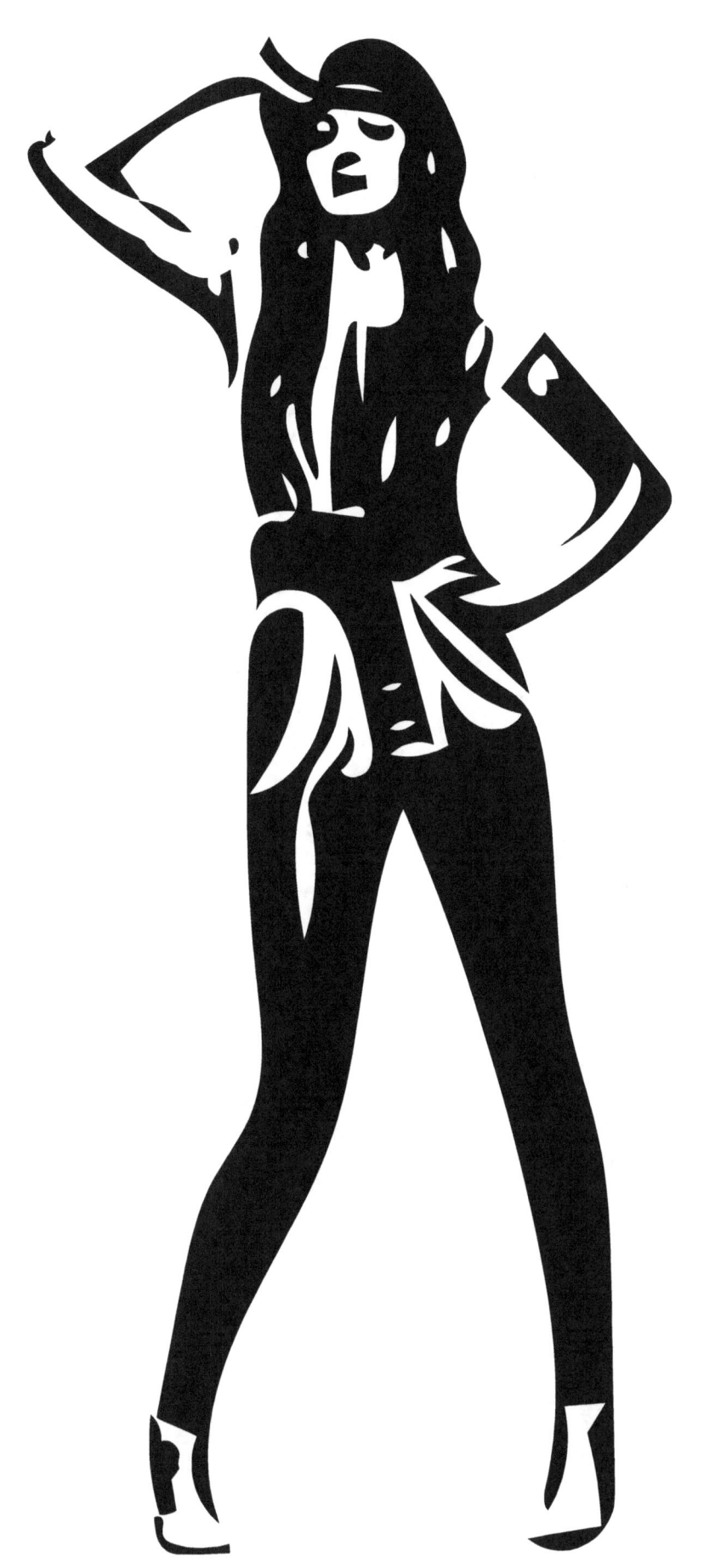

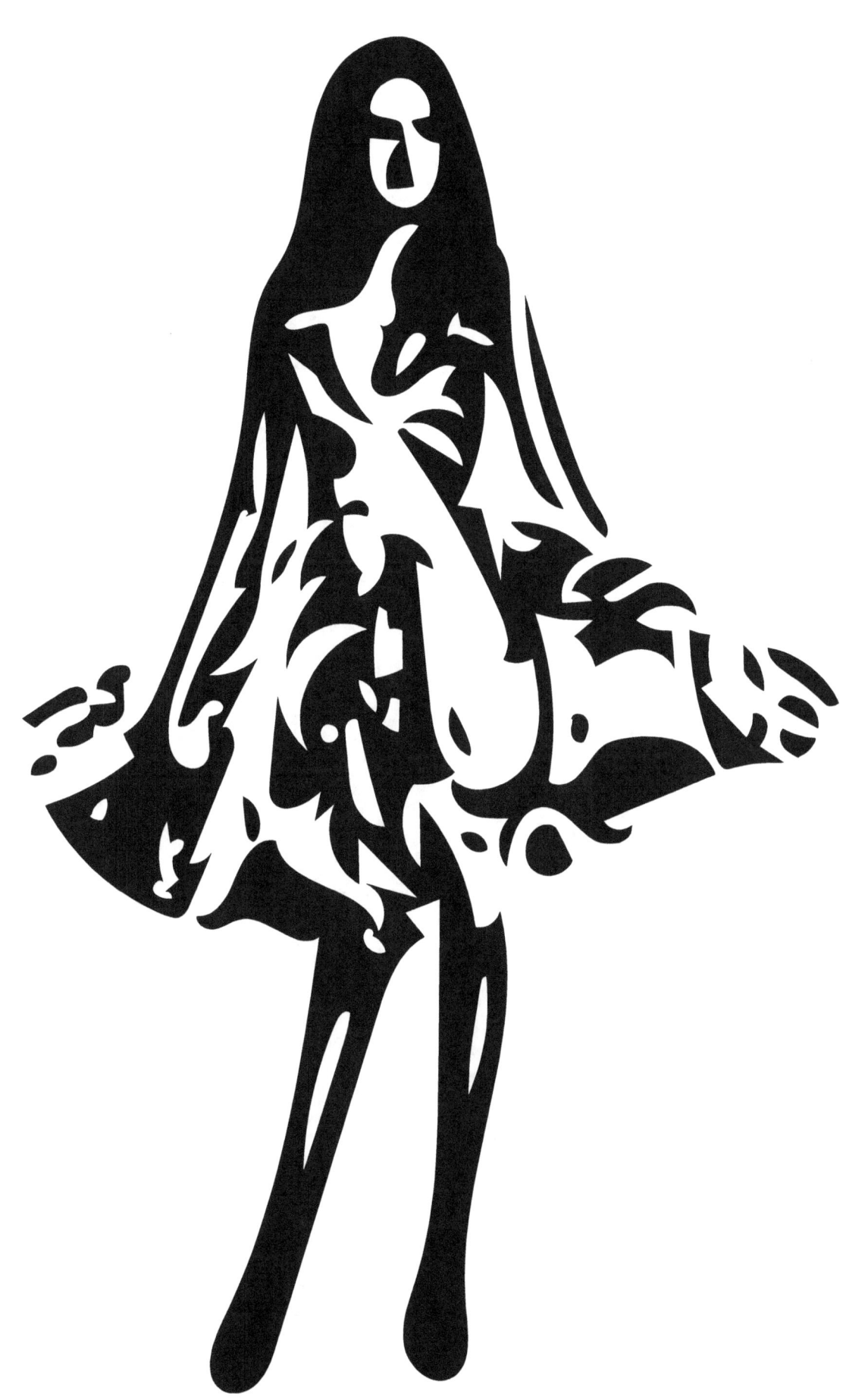

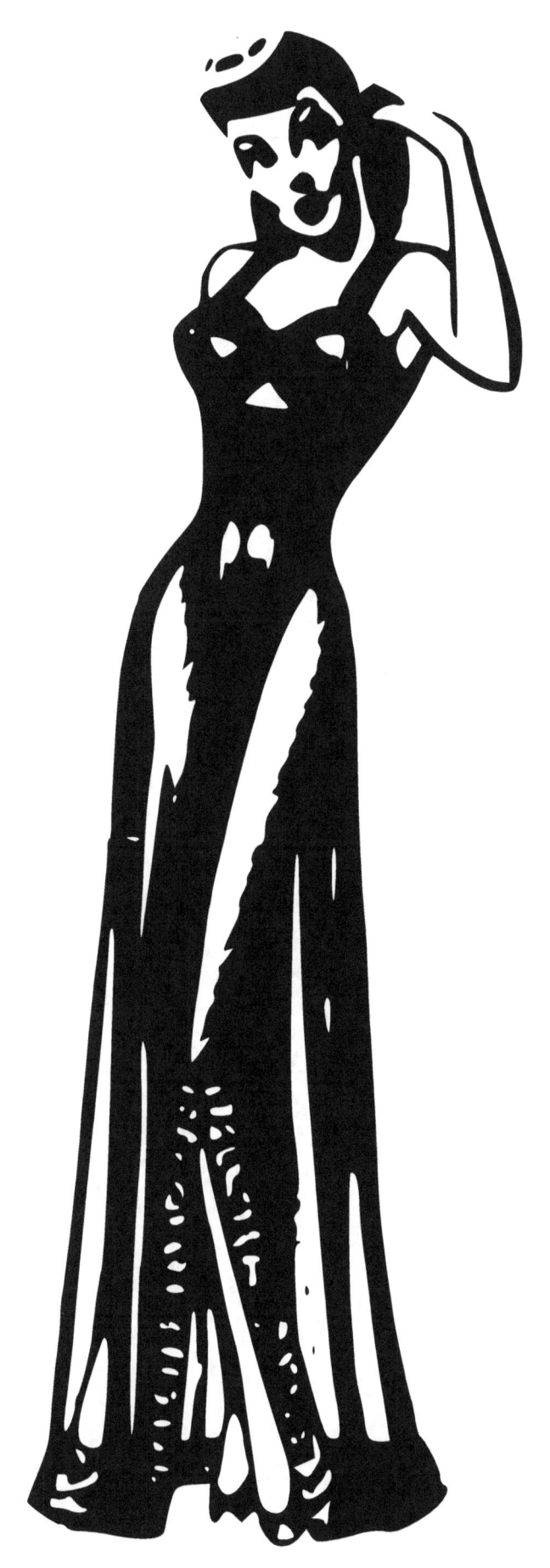

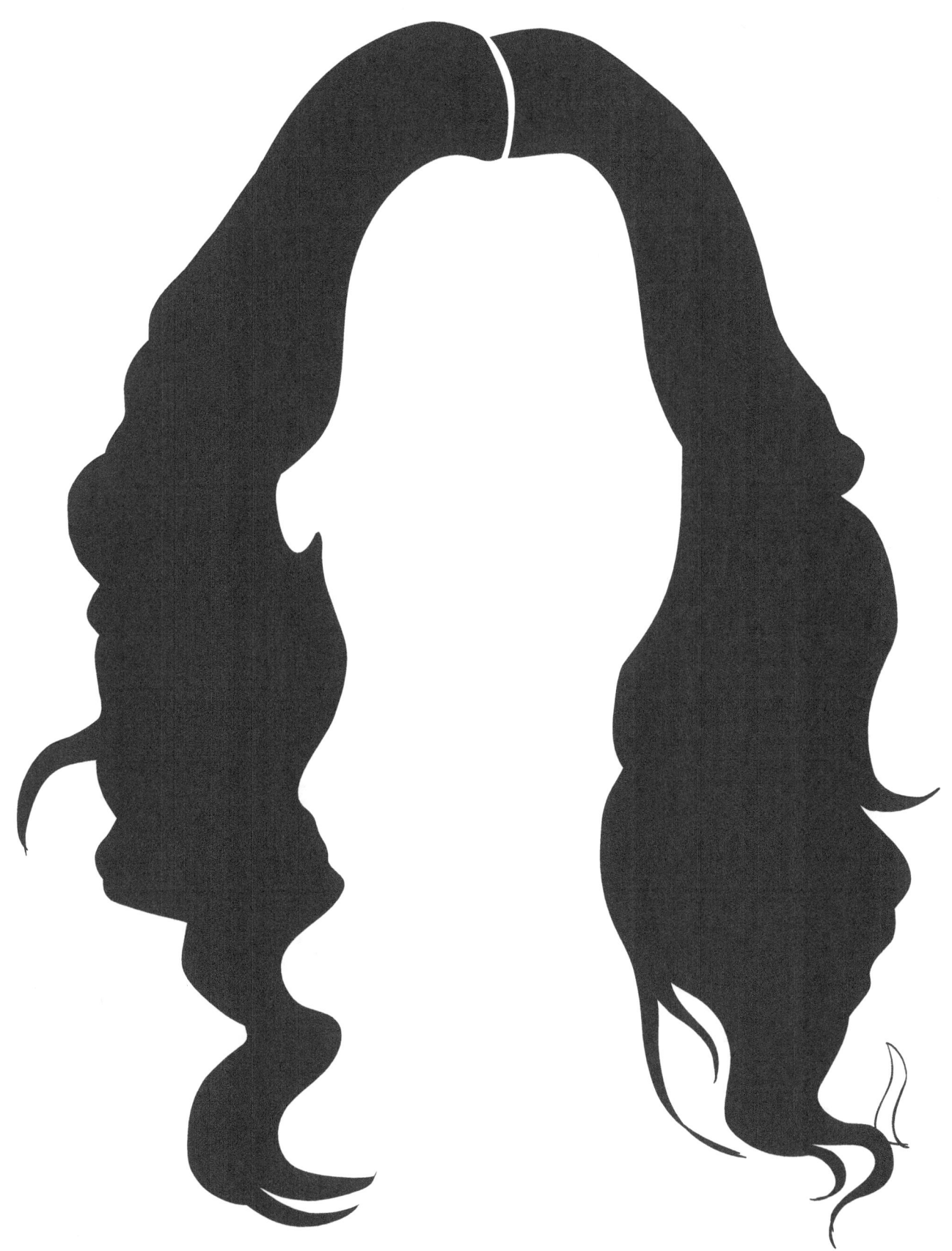

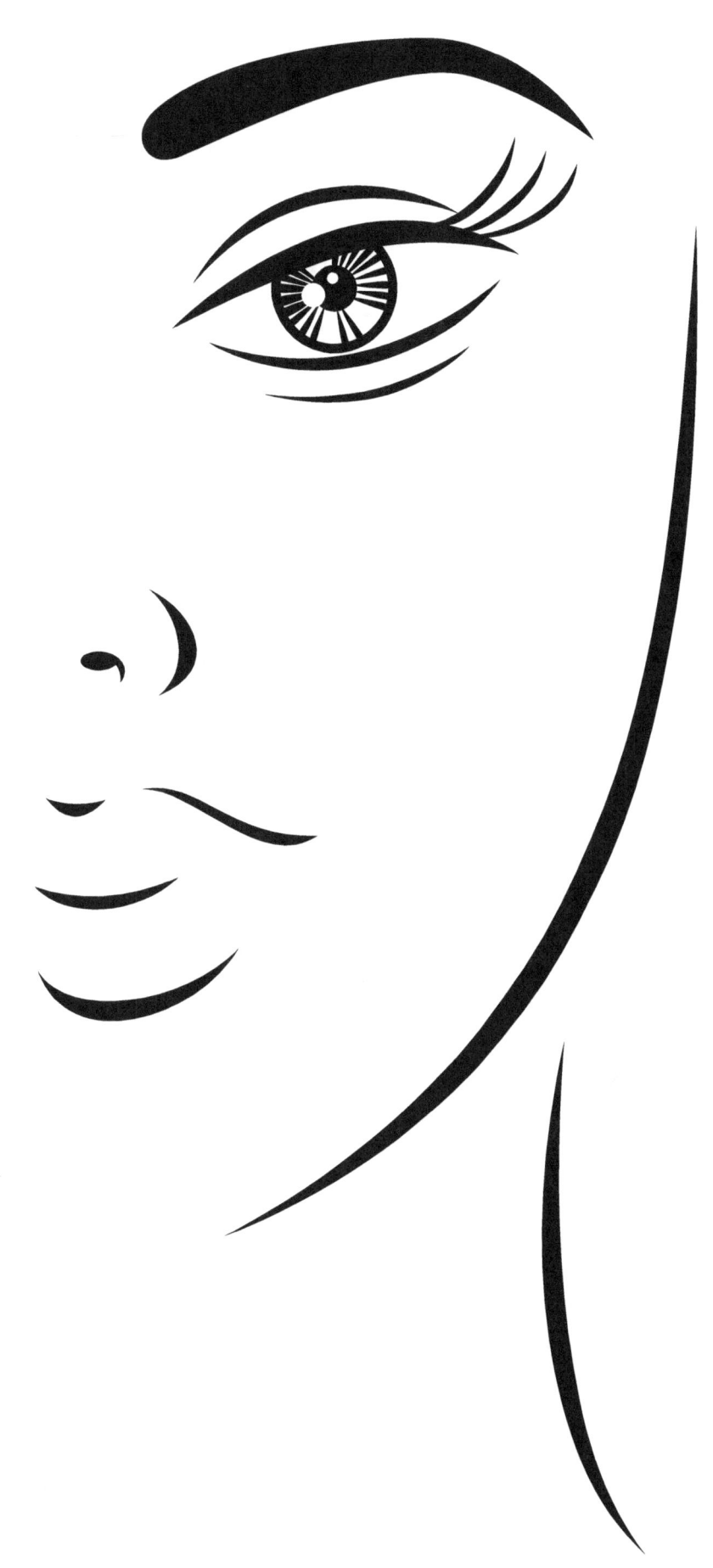

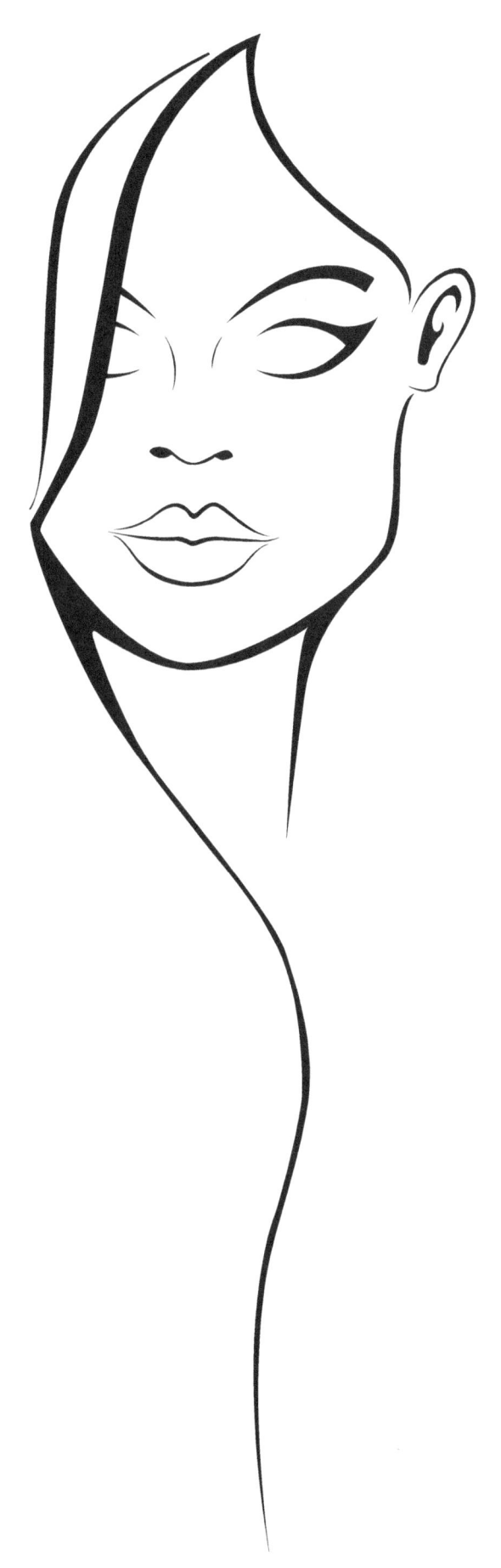

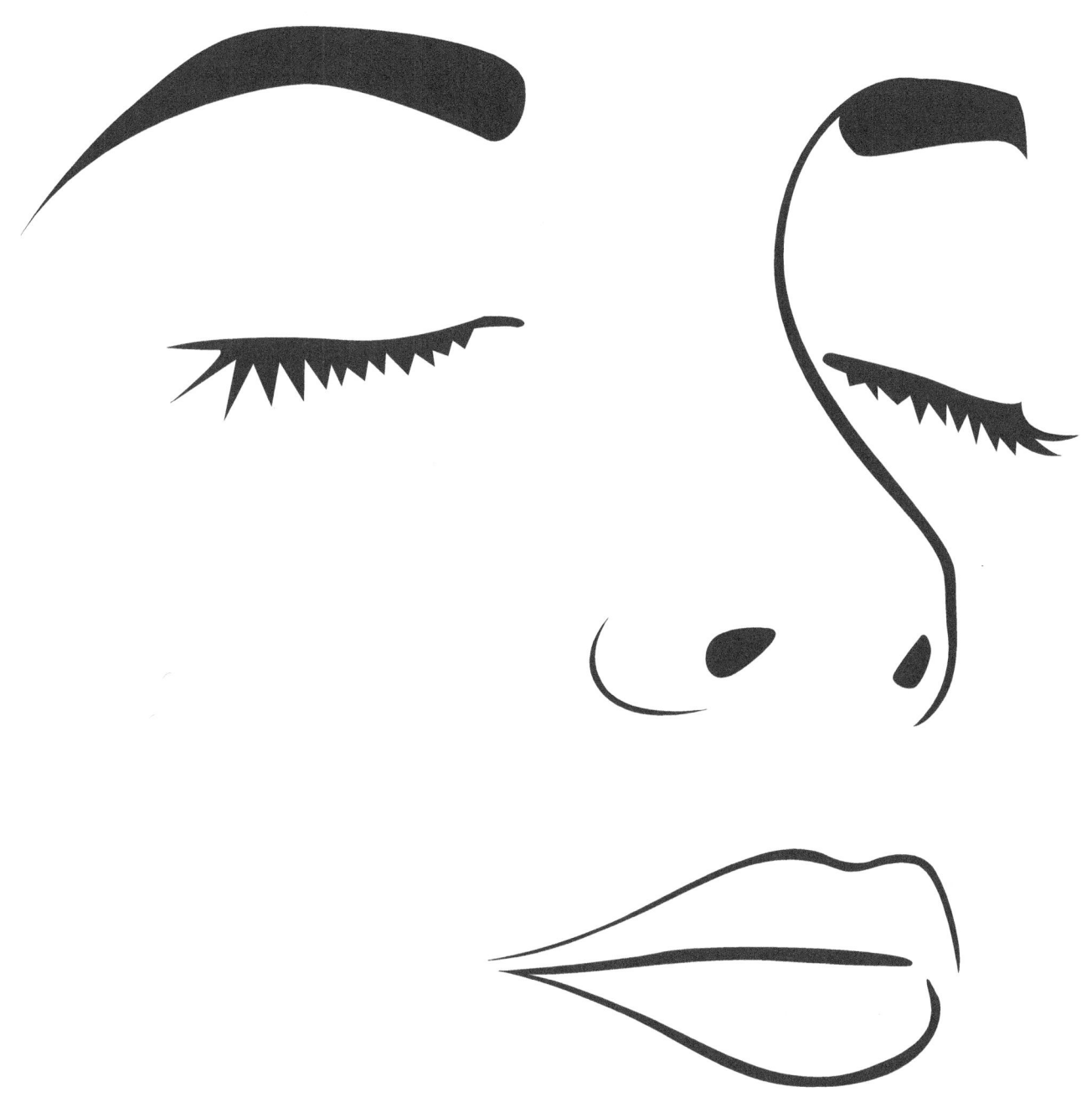

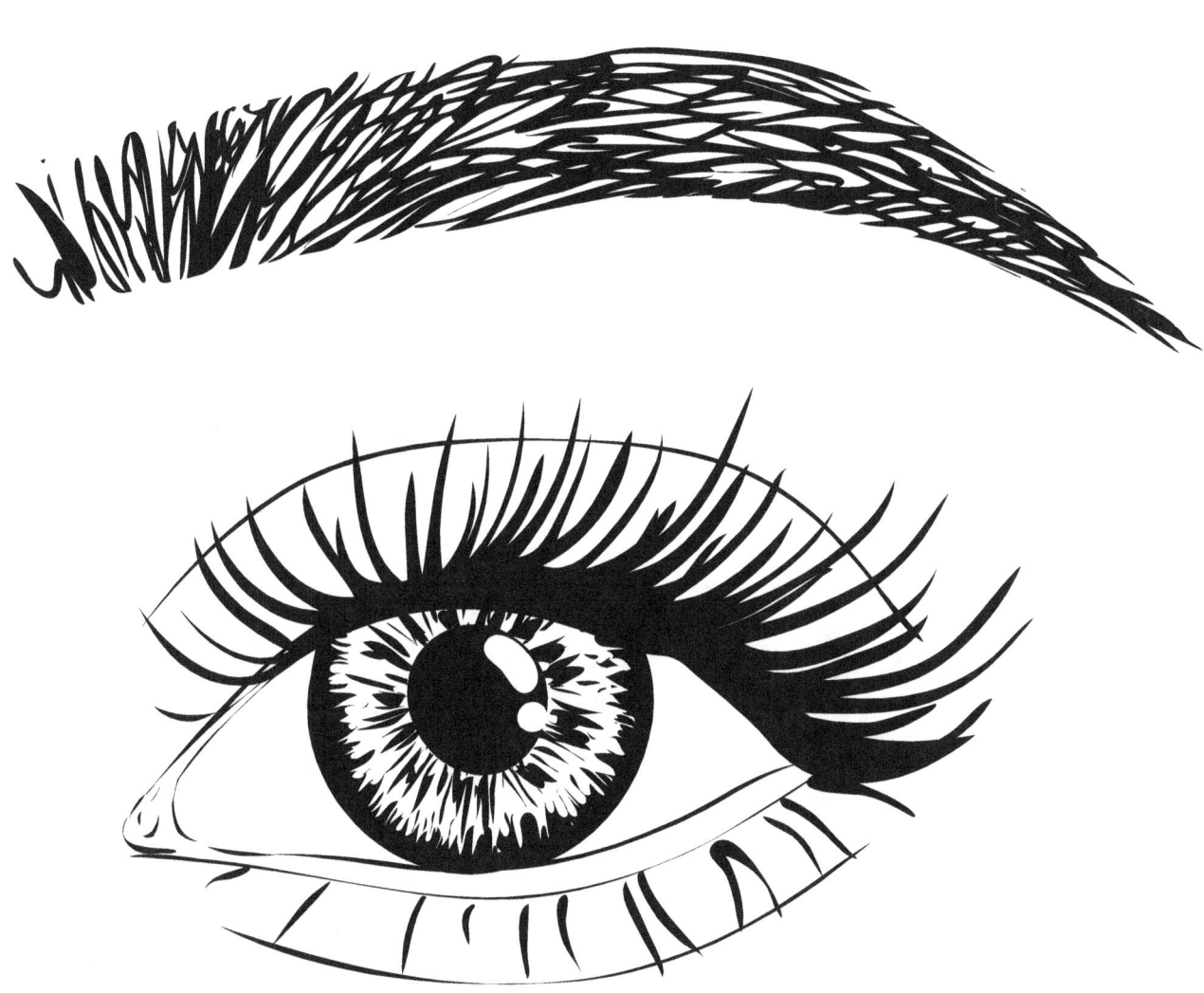

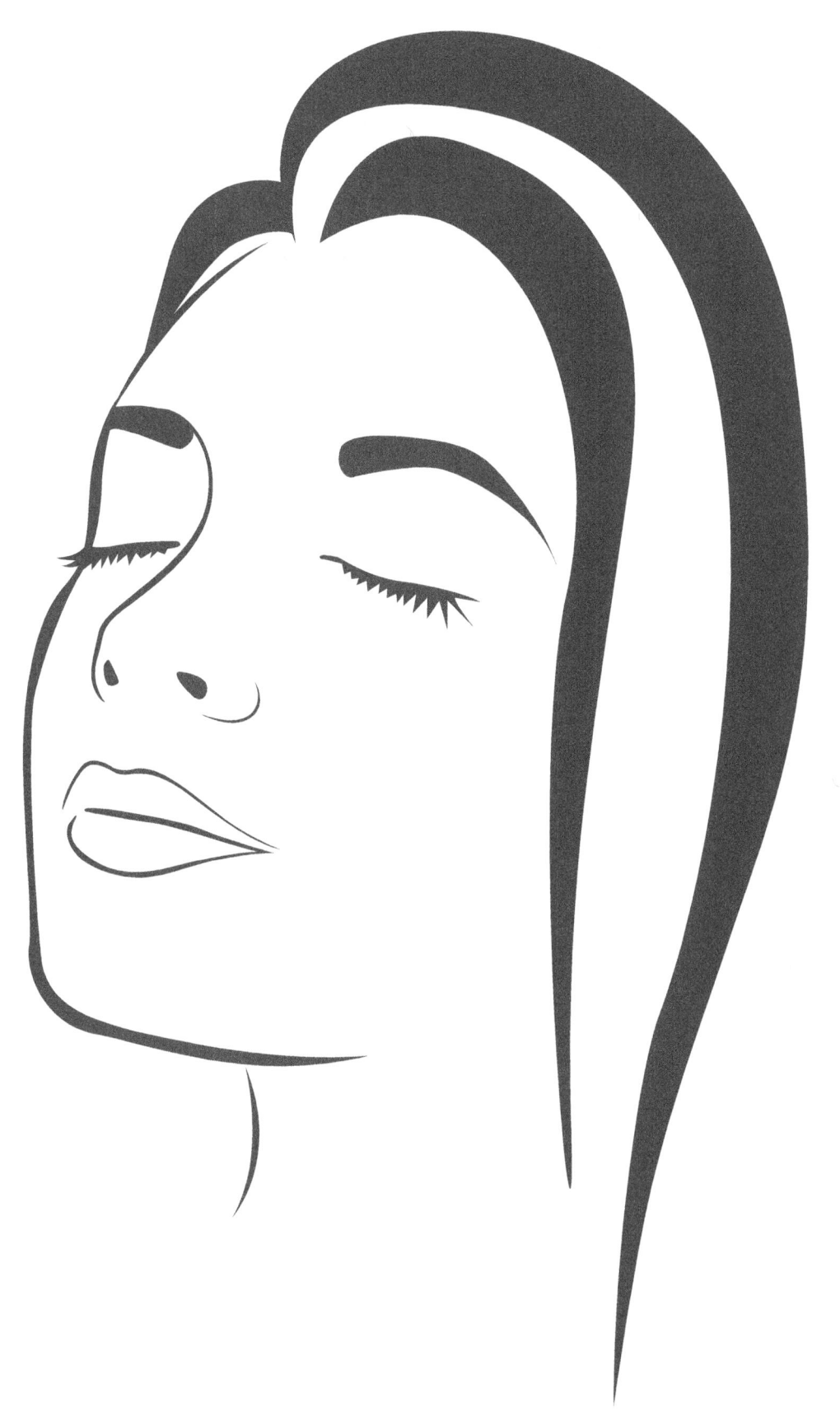

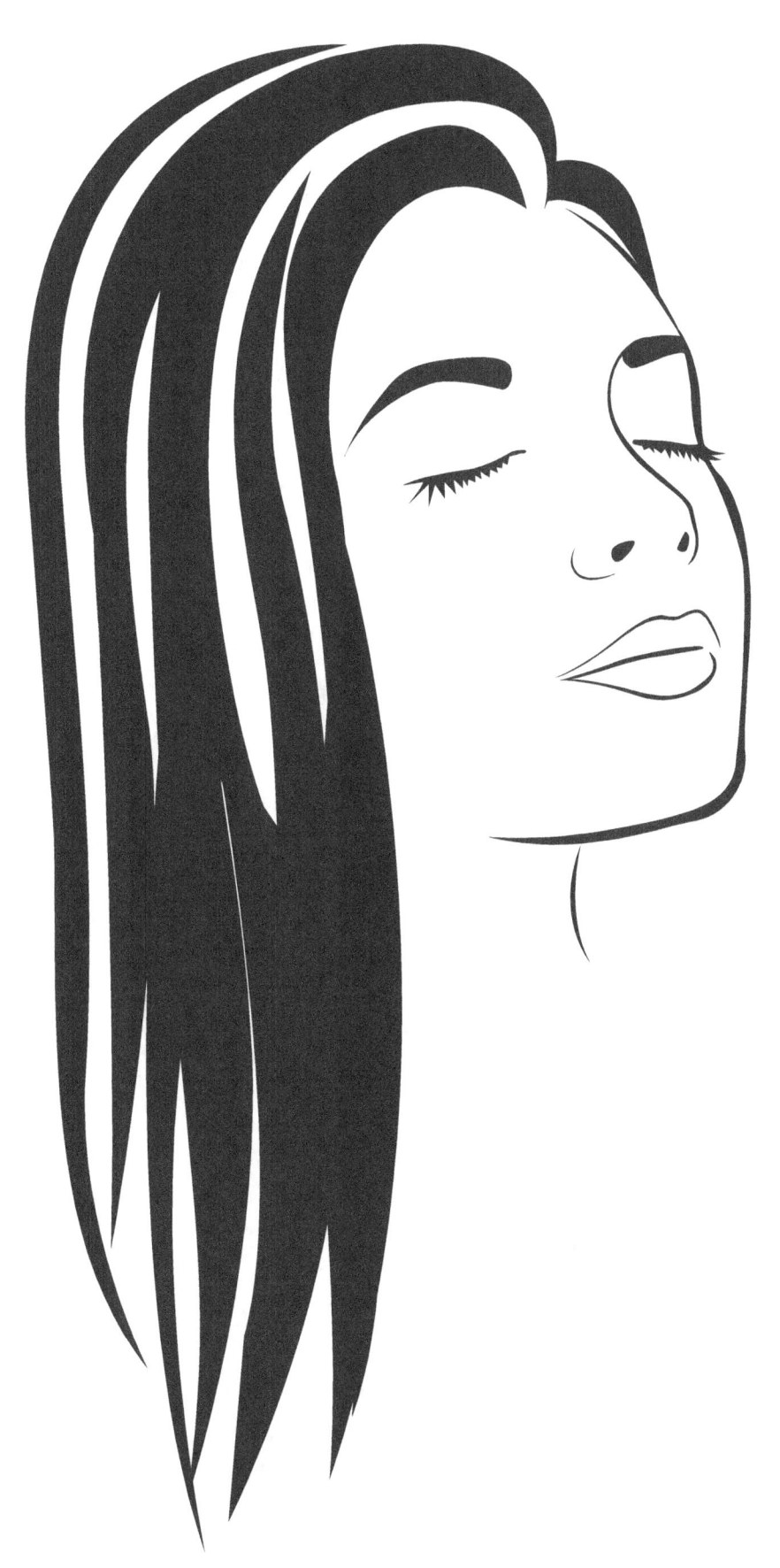

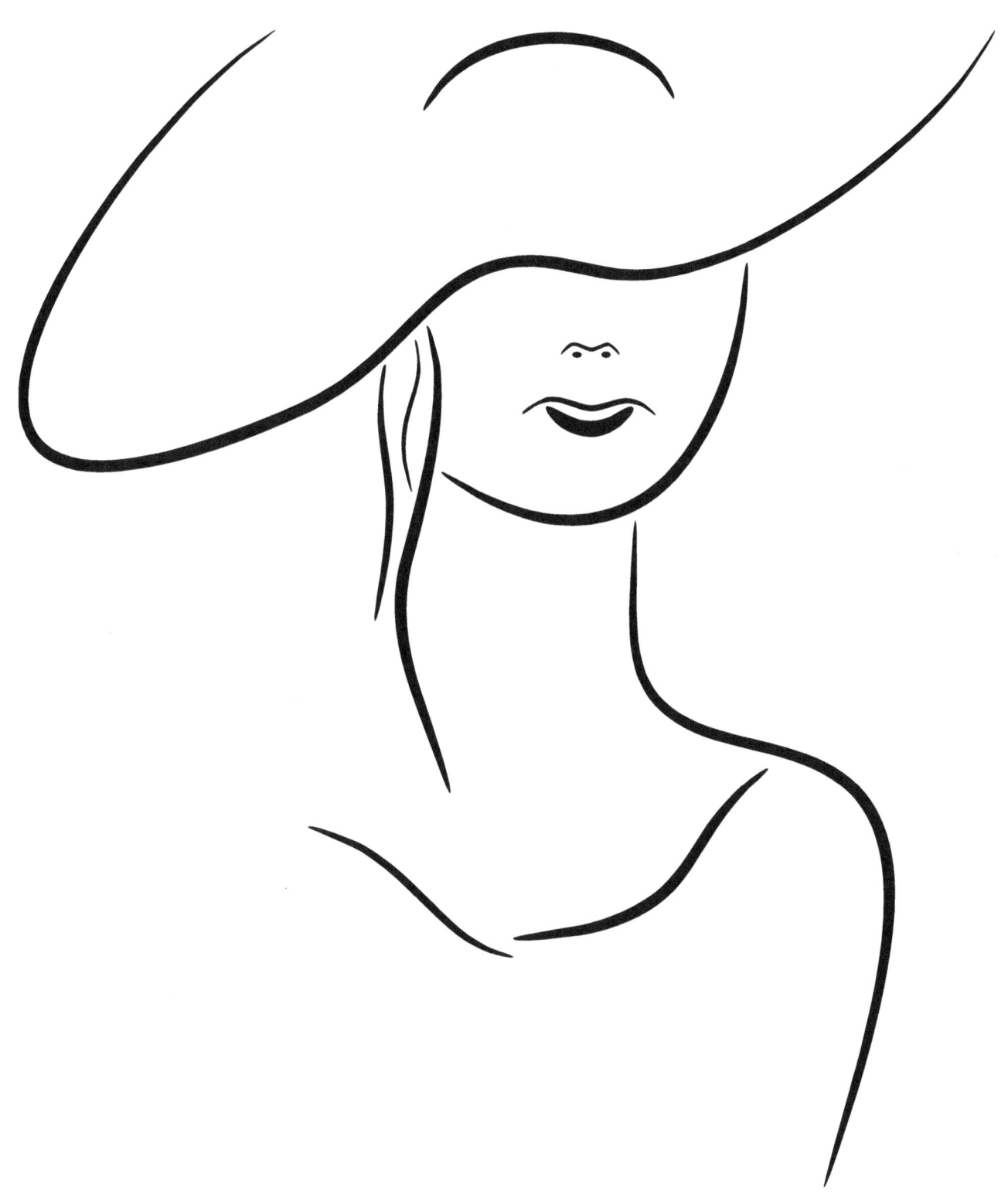

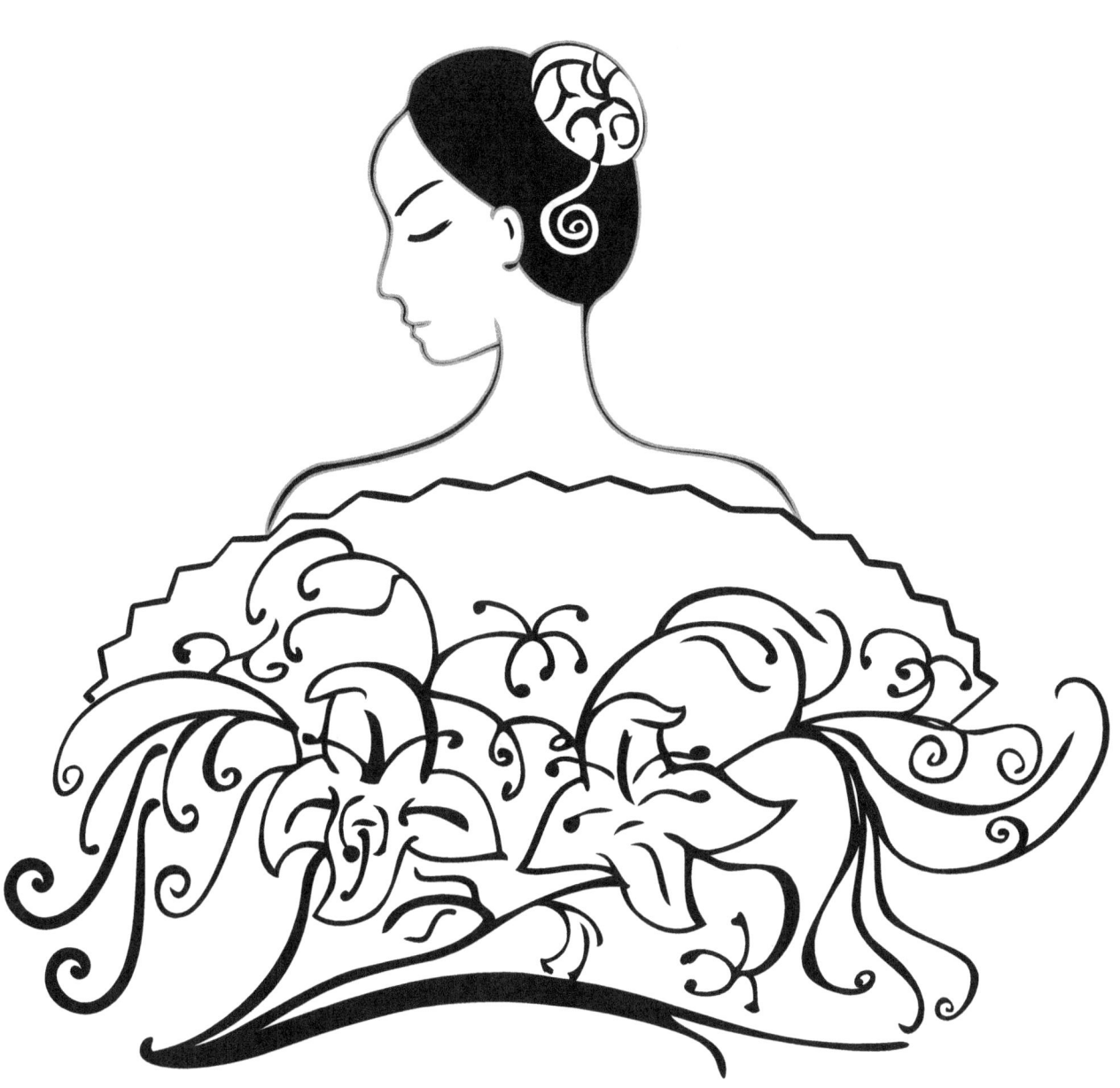

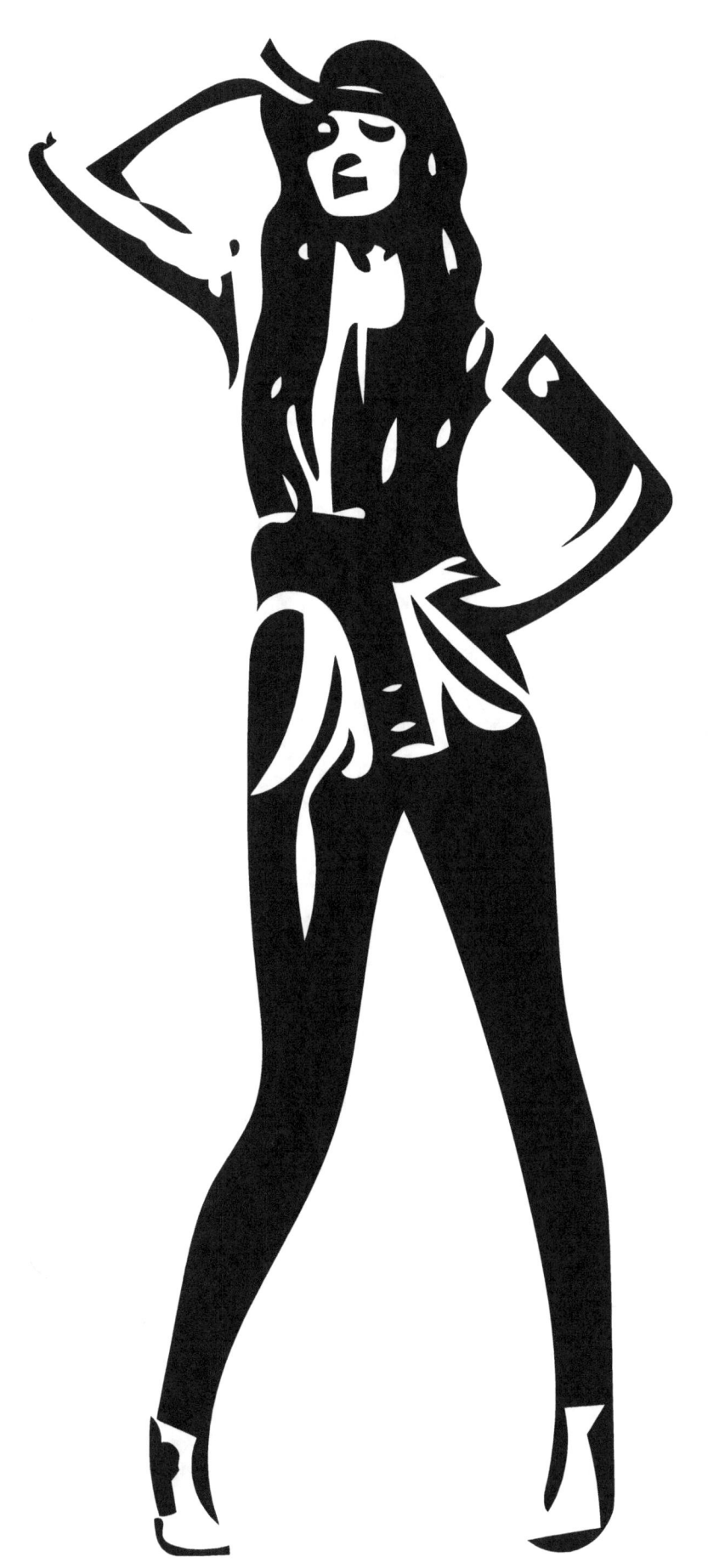

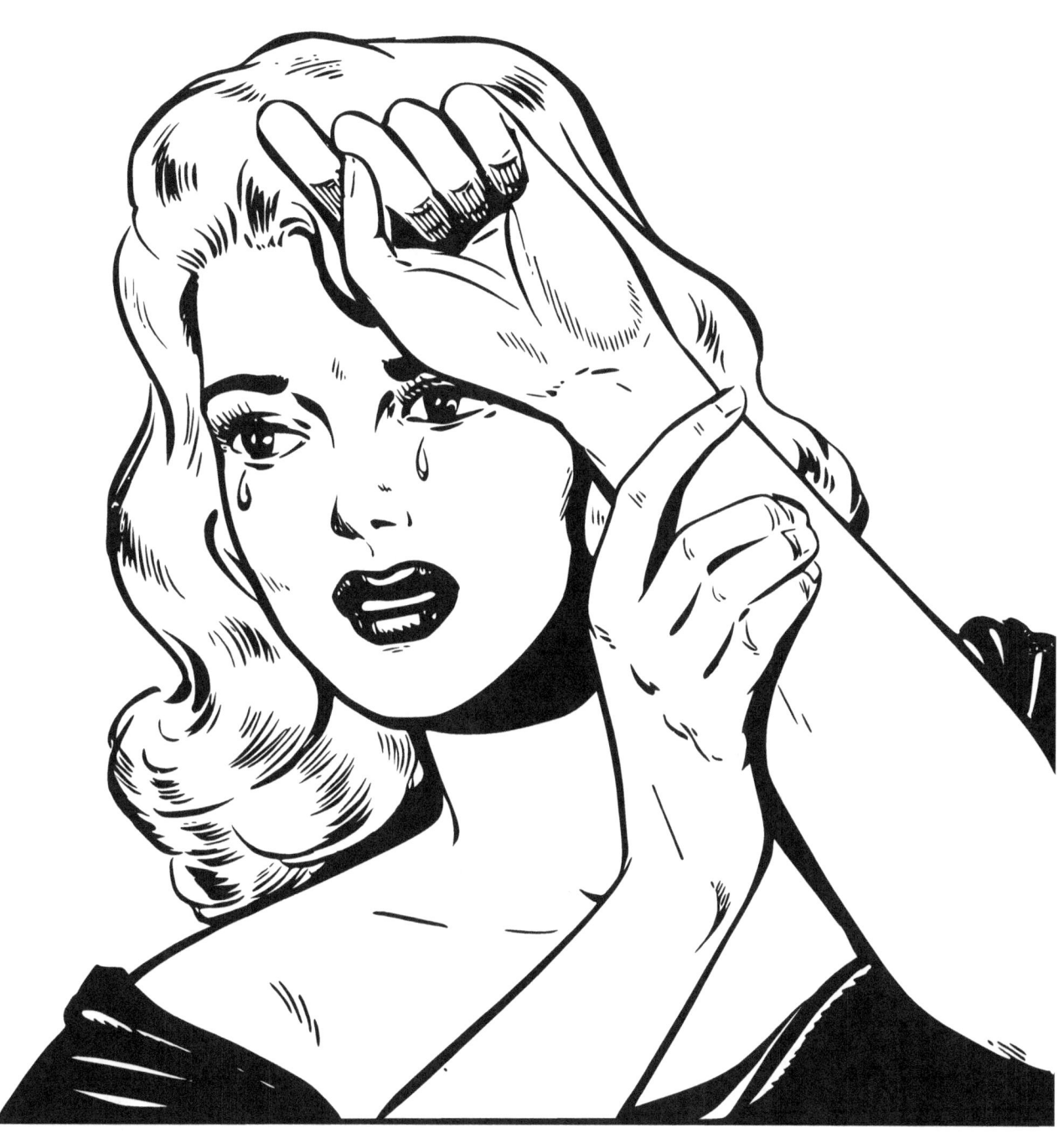

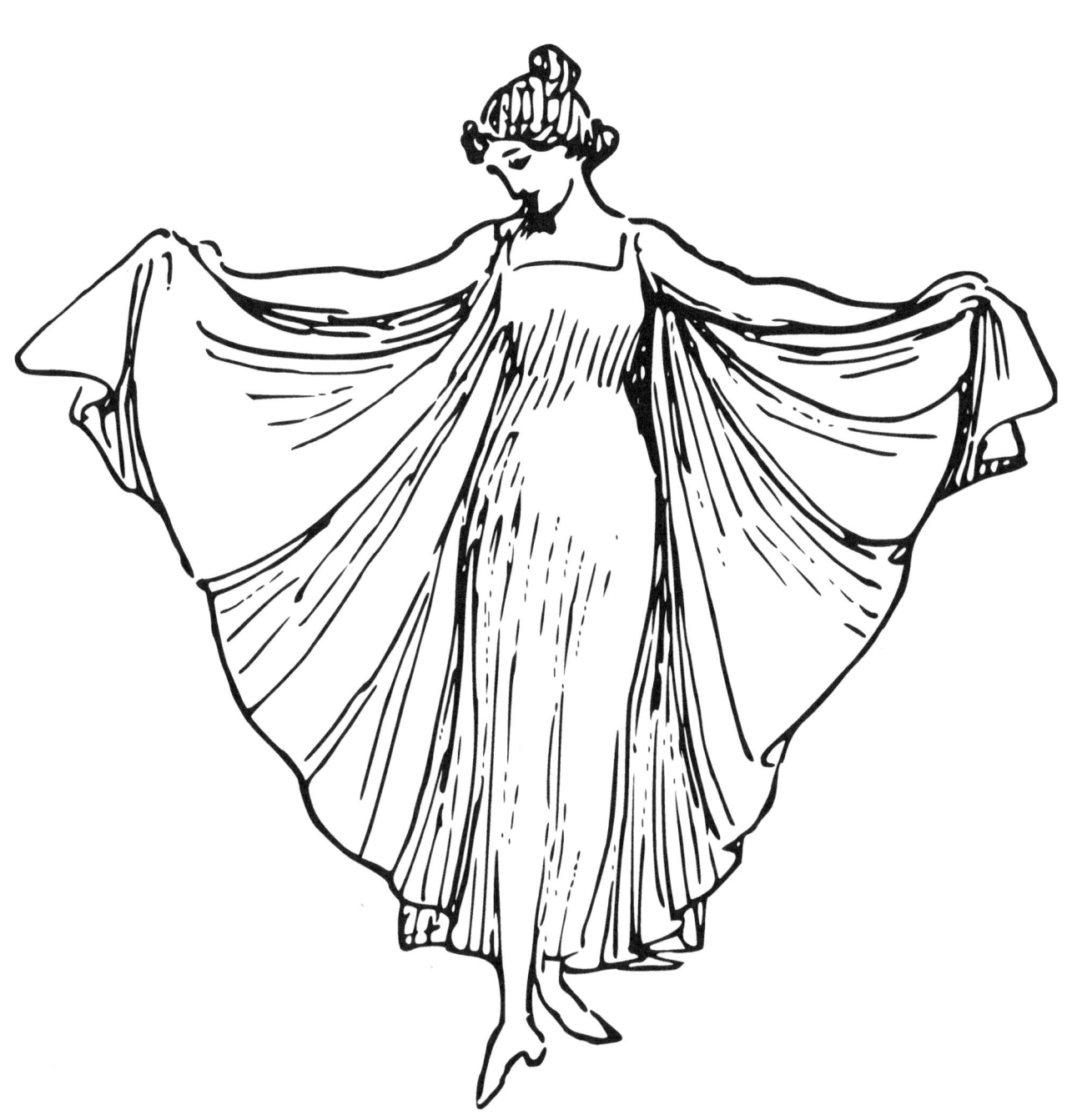

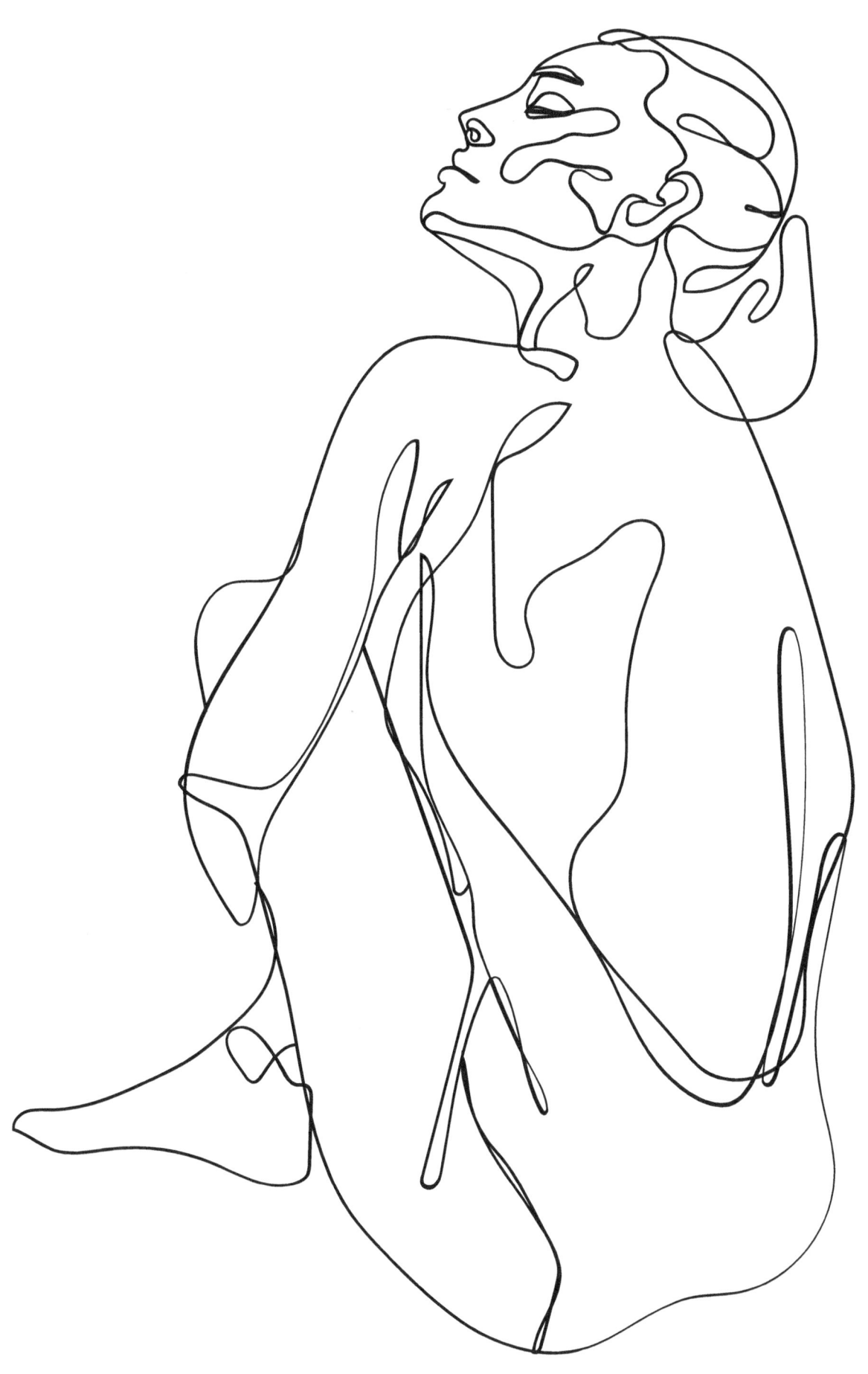

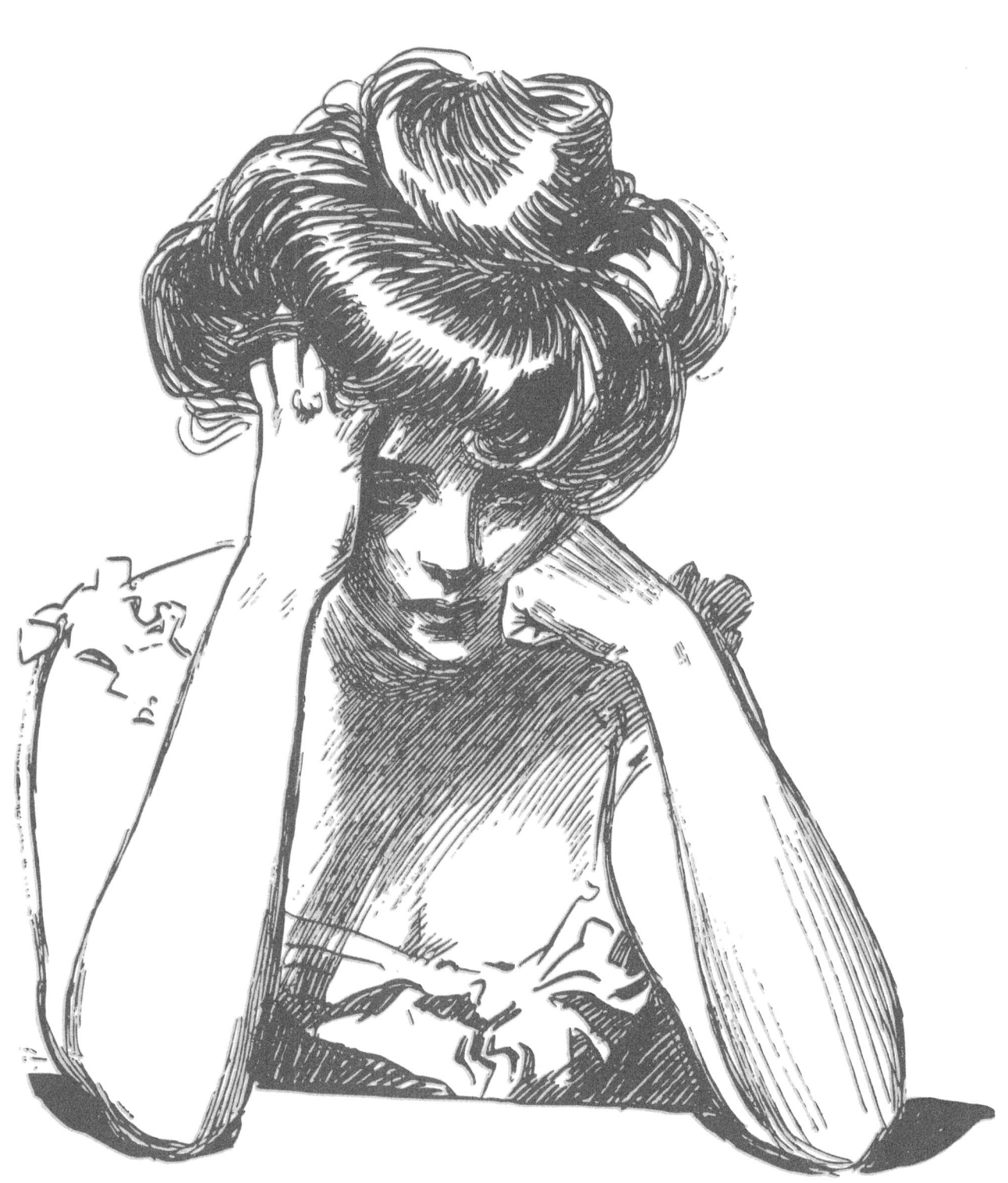

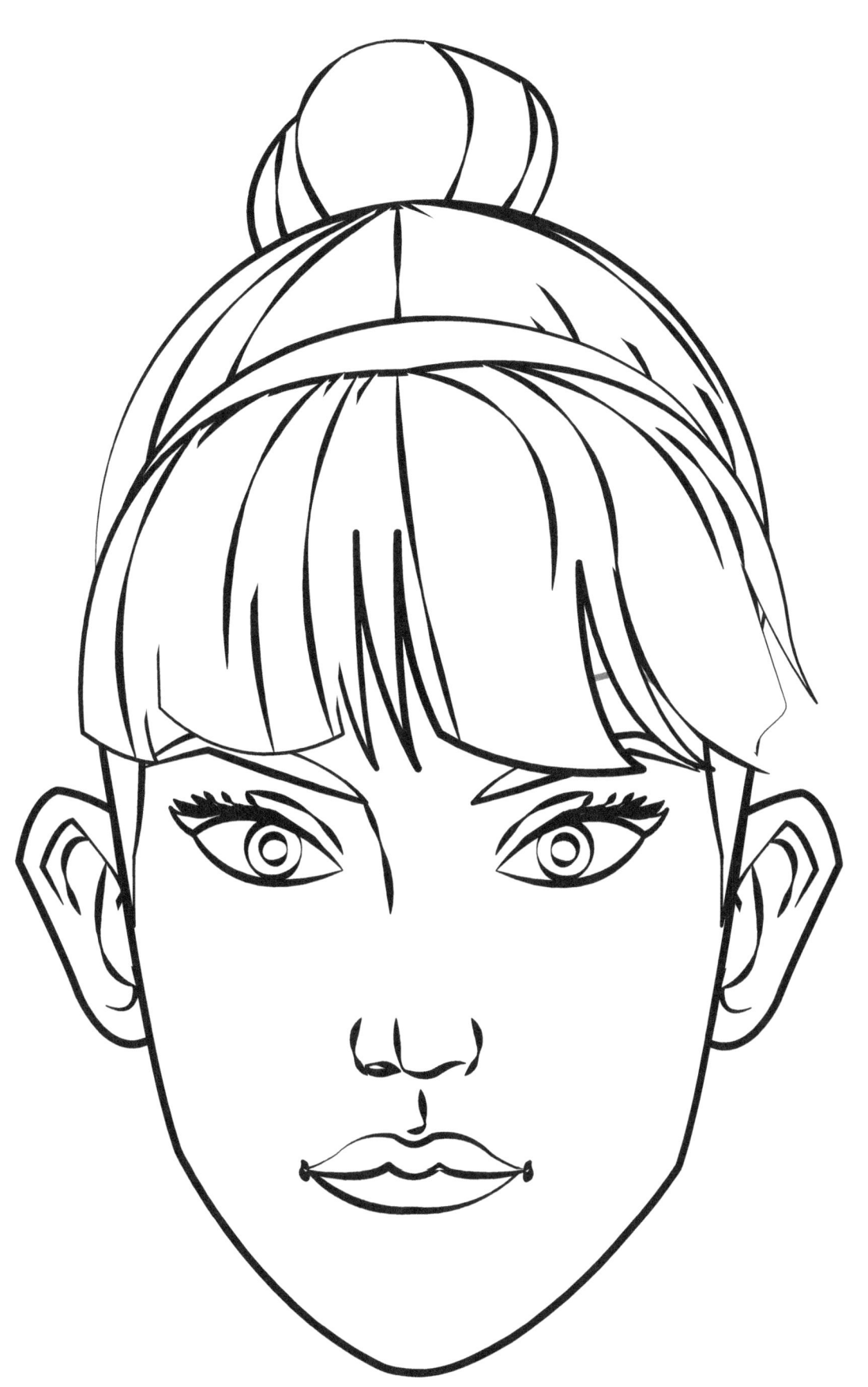

www.ingramcontent.com/pod-product-compliance
Lightning Source LLC
Chambersburg PA
CBHW081444220526
45466CB00008B/2498